CULTURE SMART!

COSTA RICA

Jane Koutnik

·K·U·P·E·R·A·R·D·

This book is available for special discounts for bulk purchases for sales promotions or premiums. Special editions, including personalized covers, excerpts of existing books, and corporate imprints, can be created in large quantities for special needs.

For more information in the USA write to Special Markets/Premium Sales, 1745 Broadway, MD 6–2, New York, NY 10019, or e-mail specialmarkets@randomhouse.com.

In the United Kingdom contact Kuperard publishers at the address below.

ISBN 978 1 85733 665 8
This book is also available as an e-book: eISBN 978 1 85733 666 5

British Library Cataloguing in Publication Data
A CIP catalogue entry for this book is available from the British Library

First published in Great Britain
by Kuperard, an imprint of Bravo Ltd
59 Hutton Grove, London N12 8DS
Tel: +44 (0) 20 8446 2440   Fax: +44 (0) 20 8446 2441
www.culturesmart.co.uk
Inquiries: sales@kuperard.co.uk

Distributed in the United States and Canada
by Random House Distribution Services
1745 Broadway, New York, NY 10019
Tel: +1 (212) 572-2844   Fax: +1 (212) 572-4961
Inquiries: csorders@randomhouse.com

Series Editor Geoffrey Chesler
Design Bobby Birchall

Printed in Malaysia

The publishers would like to thank the Costa Rica Tourist Board for permission to reproduce the images on pages 15, 17, 18, 25, 37, 38, 40, 41, 45, 76, 77, 79, 83, 90, 97, 115, 119, 124, and 127.

Images on the following pages reproduced under Creative Commons Attribution-Share Alike 3.0 Unported license: 14 © D.Hatcher/Medeis; 4 © HansenBCN; 29 © MadriCR; 43 © Peter Andersen; 49 and 142 © Lex.mercurio; 111 © Chepetoño; 130 © Eric T Gunther; 136 © Haakon S. Krohn

Reproduced under Creative Commons Attribution-Share Alike 2.0 Generic license: 13 © Ardyiii; 35 © Wendy Lefkowich; 46 © Lex.mercurio; 81 © Chad Rosenthal; 94 © Umacamera; 114 © Codo

About the Author

JANE KOUTNIK is a teacher, translator, writer, and craft jeweler who has lived in Costa Rica for nearly thirty years. After graduating in Philosophy and English from the University of California at San Diego, she traveled to Costa Rica, fell in love with the country, and decided to call it home. Over the years she has worked for mutual English–Spanish understanding in her local rural community, and has contributed to several guidebooks and tourist magazines. Her passion for the environment has led to intensive time and energy dedicated to conservation, working with the government, the local community, and environmental groups.

The Culture Smart! series is continuing to expand.
For further information and latest titles visit
www.culturesmart.co.uk

The publishers would like to thank **CultureSmart!**Consulting for its help in researching and developing the concept for this series.

CultureSmart!Consulting creates tailor-made seminars and consultancy programs to meet a wide range of corporate, public-sector, and individual needs. Whether delivering courses on multicultural team building in the USA, preparing Chinese engineers for a posting in Europe, training call-center staff in India, or raising the awareness of police forces to the needs of diverse ethnic communities, it provides essential, practical, and powerful skills worldwide to an increasingly international workforce.

For details, visit www.culturesmartconsulting.com

CultureSmart!Consulting and **CultureSmart!** guides have both contributed to and featured regularly in the weekly travel program "Fast Track" on BBC World TV.

contents

contents

Map of Costa Rica

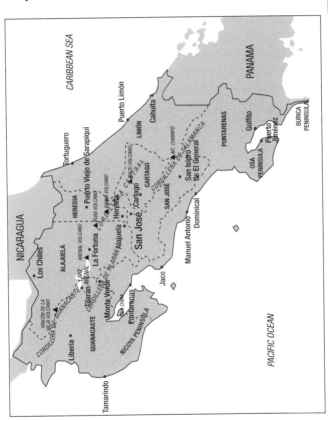

introduction

Costa Rica is renowned both for its tropical beauty and for the warmth of the "Ticos"—its people's own name for themselves. The Ticos have a wonderful enthusiasm for life, shown as much in their passion for soccer as in their demonstrations in support of human rights. They are also a proud people, who cherish their democracy in an area that has seen generations of political unrest.

Costa Ricans generally seem more European than their Central American neighbors. Though many ethnic mixtures exist, their Spanish ancestry is the most marked. The population of the Caribbean coast exhibits a blend of Afro-Caribbean, indigenous, and Chinese cultures. There has been a recent increase in immigration from Nicaragua and Colombia, adding another ingredient to the pot, and further immigration of Europeans, North Americans, and Chinese are creating a truly international mix.

There has been burgeoning development in Costa Rica over the last decade. With rapid growth, however, have come growing pains. The middle class is expanding, but there is still a significant and increasing amount of poverty in the country. The national debt has become excessive since Costa Rica leaped feet first into the competitive global economy. Free trade zones, created to encourage foreign investment, have brought in many multinational companies. Over the past few years there has been a profound movement of population to the towns of the Central Valley. Higher education is now the norm for young Ticos, which has put a strain on the national universities, and private universities have opened to meet the need. All these changes have created a challenge for the government in fulfilling the demands of development.

Culture Smart! Costa Rica aims to explore the complex human realities of modern Costa Rican life. Through the descriptions of the country's history, geography, customs, and traditions, you can see how regional differences and shared values and attitudes have developed. You will get a glimpse of the Ticos' home life, of how they do business, and of how they socialize. Armed with this information, you will be better equipped to understand your hosts and to enjoy your visit to the full. This beautiful land offers an intriguing invitation to explore and experience its diverse charms and culture. Costa Rica and the spontaneous hospitality of the Ticos await you with open arms and a smile. *Bienvenidos!*

Key Facts

Official Name	República de Costa Rica (Republic of Costa Rica)	
Capital City	San José	Pop. 300,000 approx
Population	4,576,572 (2012)	
Area	19,730 square miles (51,100 square km.)	
Geography	Situated in the heart of the Central American isthmus, which connects North and South America	Bordered to the north by Nicaragua, to the southeast by Panama, to the west by the Pacific Ocean, and to the east by the Atlantic Ocean
Terrain	A backbone of volcanoes and mountains through the center divides the Pacific and Atlantic slopes. Two coastlines of tropical beaches, lowland rain forests, high-altitude cloud forests, humid, verdant northern plains, and the "dry" savannahs of Guanacaste create a broad diversity.	
Climate	Tropical. There are two seasons, the wet season, *invierno* (winter), May-Nov., and the dry season, *verano* (summer), Dec.-April.	Altitude greatly affects climatic conditions and temperatures.
Currency	The *colon*, which devalues annually about 10 percent.	In 2012, US $1.00 equalled 505 *colones*.
Ethnic Makeup	There is a wide diversity of ethnicity: Spanish and other European countries, North American, Chinese, indigenous groups, and Afro-Caribbeans.	

Language	Spanish. A few indigenous languages are still spoken, but almost exclusively on the indigenous reservations.	English is increasingly used in the tourism and business industries.
Government	Democratic Republic. A constitutional democracy with a unicameral legislative assembly directly elected every four years.	There are seven provinces, each electing deputies to the legislative assembly.
Religion	Roman Catholicism is the official state religion.	There is a growing number of Christian denominations and a Jewish community. Tolerance prevails.
Media	There are state and autonomous television channels, as well as private channels. Cable TV and Direct TV are widely available.	The national newspapers include the daily *La Nación*, *La Republica*, *Al Día*, and *La Prensa Libre*.
Media: English Language	The *Tico Times* newspaper is published weekly and on-line at www.ticotimes.net.	Another news site is www.amcostarica.com. There are numerous English tourist magazines.
Electricity	110 volts and 220 volts (60 Hz)	
Video/TV	NTSC system	
Internet Domain	.cr	
Telephone	The country code is 506.	To dial out of the country, dial 00.
Time	GMT -6 hours	

chapter one

LAND & PEOPLE

A GEOGRAPHICAL SNAPSHOT

Costa Rica, the third-smallest republic (after
El Salvador and Belize) of Central America, is
located on the narrow isthmus connecting North
and South America. It is bordered to the north by
Nicaragua and to the southeast by Panama; the
Pacific Ocean washes the western coast, and the
Atlantic Ocean, or Caribbean Sea, laps its eastern
shore. This small country is situated in the tropics,
between 8° and 11° North latitude and between
83° and 85° West longitude.

A backbone of volcanoes and mountains
extends north to south, the ranges, or *cordilleras*,
being an extension of the Andes Sierra Madre
chain. There are four distinct mountain ranges—
Guanacaste and Tilarán in the north, Central and
Talamanca to the south. As a live part of the Pacific
"Rim of Fire," Costa Rica is home to seven of the
isthmus's forty-two active volcanoes. Earth tremors
and small quakes that shake the country are not an
unusual occurrence. Many dormant or extinct
cones are also dotted along the mountain ranges.

The country is divided into seven provinces:
San José, Heredia, Alajuela, and Cartago, whose
capital cities make up the central valley;

Guanacaste, along the northwestern area of the country; Puntarenas, which runs from the center of the Pacific coast south; and Limón, which covers the Caribbean coast and is characterized by its Afro-Caribbean culture.

The highest point of the country is Mount Chirripó, which rises majestically to 12,532 feet (3,820 meters). Its amazing vistas, fresh air, cloud forests, and high, treeless plateau, or paramo, are all protected under the national park network.

The *Meseta Central,* a high-altitude plain, occupies the heart of the country. San José, the capital, is located in the center, surrounded by the neighboring cities of Heredia, Alajuela, and Cartago. Almost two-thirds of the population live in this small, fertile valley, surrounded by the majestic Irazú, Poás, and Barva volcanoes. The verdant foothills above the city yield premium-quality, high-altitude coffee, exotic flowers for export, and a wide variety of vegetables. The countryside is dotted with abundant dairy farms,

which produce delicious cheeses and other fresh dairy products. Above the pastures, protected areas help to conserve the cloud forests that drape the mountaintops and are home to the distinctive red and green *quetzal* bird.

Costa Rica's world-renowned tropical beaches continue to seduce both national and international visitors. The Pacific and Caribbean coasts, each with its unique beauty and characteristics, make up about 621 miles (1,000 km) of shoreline. The Pacific coastal plain is generally narrower than its Caribbean counterpart, with some steep cliffs.

The northern Caribbean area offers an intriguing network of waterways to explore. The canal system was officially inaugurated in 1974 to improve access to the northeast for economic development. Artificial canals account for only about 20 percent of the system; the rest is rivers and lagoons, which were connected to open the waterways for navigation. Both coasts provide turtle-nesting areas at certain times throughout the year. The distinctive colors of the sandy coastline range from glistening white to shimmering black, and luxury hotels contrast with wild, undeveloped beaches.

The world-class rivers have drawn interest from eco- and adventure tourists, seeking either a tranquil downstream float to explore wildlife and exotic plants or an adrenalin rush, rafting the white water. These vital veins of the country have been respected as a true national treasure, though much work remains to be done to conserve these vulnerable natural resources. The Costa Ricans support ecotourism as an economically sustainable venture that protects their natural patrimony for themselves and future generations.

The great natural diversity created by Costa Rica's varied topography invites the visitor to explore and experience this nature-lover's paradise. There is something here for everyone, and the Ticos—the Costa Ricans—are proud to show off their beautiful country.

CLIMATE

Costa Rica has a tropical climate, modified by topography. The country has two seasons, the wet season, or *invierno* (winter), generally between May and November, and the dry season, *verano* (summer), from December to April. The wet season is characterized by sunny mornings followed by torrential downpours later in the day. There are occasional *temporales* throughout the rainy season. These consist of continual drizzles, usually lasting a few days. The wet season has become known as the "green season" in the tourist industry. On the Caribbean coast the dry season tends to be shorter, though September and October are usually the driest months there, when the rest of the country is experiencing its wettest weather. The Pacific northwestern area of Guanacaste is characterized by the driest climate in the country, though it too has a well-defined rainy season.

The dry season brings clear skies, sunny days, and breezes. December can be outright windy, with its famous north winds. *Pelo de gato*, or "cat's hair," is a fine mist that is blown down over the mountain slopes at this time of year, and afternoon rainbows over the mountains add to the magic. Clear, windy nights in the summer months can bring quite cool temperatures to the Central Valley and surrounding mountains. Temperatures vary little between the seasons, the main influence on temperature being altitude. Both coasts are generally very hot and humid, with the Caribbean coast being a few degrees cooler than the Pacific.

The lowland plains are also hot and humid. As you climb, the temperature cools. In one of the coldest spots, Mount Chirripó, it is not unusual to have morning frost and sheets of ice covering the small lakes. The mean temperature for San José, situated at 3,691 feet (1,125 meters), is a comfortable 75°F (24°C).

These near-perfect conditions contribute to the agreeable nature of the Ticos. Because they do not have to fight the elements for survival, they can focus on enjoying their idyllic climate.

A BRIEF HISTORY

It would take several volumes to do justice to Costa Rica's history. This brief overview aims simply to connect the dots and show how the Ticos' particular history and experience have resulted in a peaceful nation of proud, self-reliant individuals.

Pre-Columbian Era

Human habitation has been traced back at least 10,000 years in this land of mountains and swampy lowlands. Long before Columbus arrived on its Caribbean shores, a substantial indigenous population, consisting of many politically fragmented tribes, with distinct customs and

cultures, separated the two great high civilizations of Mesoamerica to the north and the Andes to the south. Today, there is little evidence of the pre-Columbian monumental architecture found in other parts of the isthmus, though archaeologists

continue to unearth interesting remains. The indigenous Caribs along the Caribbean seaboard, and the Borucas and Chibchas in the Pacific southwest, were seminomadic hunters and fishermen who cultivated tubers and lived in communal villages. These Caribbean and southwestern tribes were influenced by South American cultures. The Chibchas were responsible for the perfectly spherical granite balls, of unknown purpose, that are found at burial sites throughout the region. The southwestern tribes became highly skilled workers in jade and gold, creating some exquisite designs and artifacts.

Guayabo, on the slopes of the Turrialba volcano in Cartago province, is the country's largest archaeological site. The area now being excavated has been continuously inhabited from about 1500 BCE. At its peak, the ancient stone city, dating from 1000 BCE to 1400 CE, is believed to have had 10,000 inhabitants. Excavations continue to shed light on these mysterious indigenous people.

The Corobicis inhabited the highland valleys, as did the Nahuatl, who arrived from Mexico. Pottery and metalworking make up the most interesting archaeological finds throughout the country. The tribes in both the highland valleys and the Nicoya Peninsula were highly influenced by Mexican cultures.

The Chorotegas, still on the Nicoya Peninsula on the northwest coast, are today the most numerous group of the indigenous people. Their culture resembled that of the Aztecs of Mexico. They cultivated corn, lived in well-planned towns, and produced artistic sculpture and polychrome ceramics. They continue to make beautiful pottery today for the tourist trade.

The Colonial Era

In 1502, Christopher Columbus, on his fourth and last voyage, arrived at the Caribbean shores of Costa Rica, landing at Cariari, today's city of Puerto Limón. He was welcomed and treated with great hospitality by the natives, whose gifts of gold made a great—and misleading—impression on the Spanish. It wasn't long before the native Indians felt threatened by these uninvited guests, and tension mounted between them. The *conquistadores'* attempts to settle and reap the benefits of the supposedly *costa rica*, or "rich coast," were basically miserable failures. Harassed by hostile Indians, the Spanish were defeated by floods, swamps, and tropical diseases in the sweltering lowlands. For the next four decades the indigenous population was virtually left alone.

In the early 1560s the Spanish tried again to colonize and forcibly convert this region of the New World. This time the indigenous population succumbed to war, reprisal, relocation, and brutal exploitation, and to diseases such as smallpox and measles, introduced by the Europeans, against which they had no immunity. The survivors of these ravages took refuge in the remote valleys on the southeastern slopes of the Talamanca Mountains. Only the Chorotegas on the Nicoya Peninsula managed to maintain a significant indigenous presence.

Settlement

In 1562 Juan Vásquez de Coronado founded the first lasting Spanish settlement. His policies—relatively humane treatment of the surviving indigenous population, and relocating the remaining Spanish settlers to the fertile Cartago Valley in the *Meseta Central*—proved successful. The Spaniards adapted well to the cooler climate of the central highlands, where they cultivated the rich, volcanic soil and soon

became a self-sufficient rural community. King Philip II of Spain had granted the colonists the right to parcel up the land and establish the *encomienda* system of bonded labor, but without abundant native labor, or the mineral resources to develop to enable them to import slaves, the settlers were forced to work the land themselves. Their settlements were small, isolated, and slow to grow. Cartago was established as the first capital in 1563. Nearly a century after its founding there was little more than a single church surrounded by a small community of adobe (sun-dried brick) houses. All this was destroyed in the volcanic eruption of Irazú in 1723. Eventually settlements grew up around the churches of Heredia (1706), San José (1736), and Alajuela (1782). While the gentry formed a governing class in the towns, the scattered, hardy, farming communities developed an independence of spirit.

Owing to its smallness, remoteness, and lack of mineral wealth, Costa Rica was by and large left to govern itself, with taxes and salaries administered through Nicaragua. The seeds of a sound agricultural economy had been planted, and Costa Ricans were on their way to developing an individualistic and egalitarian society, based on rural democracy.

In the Pacific northwest, the Nicoya Peninsula, and the rest of Guanacaste there were large cattle farms, similar to the rest of Nicaragua. Large estate owners began to import African slaves to work on the farms.

Along the Caribbean coast, cacao plantations proved to be a profitable endeavor. This industry became well established and flourished through the years. Later tobacco would become another important crop, as well as coconuts and bananas.

In 1665 Spain closed Costa Rica's ports because of English piracy, which put an end to legal seaborne trade. As a result smuggling flourished, and this illicit trade further weakened the central colonial authority and strengthened the colonists' independent spirit. Central American colonial unity weakened as the Spanish empire's power declined in the eighteenth century. Spain lost interest and was unable to maintain the administrative structure that controlled its distant colonies. The *coup de grâce* came when Napoleon invaded Spain in 1808 and installed his brother on the Spanish throne. Costa Rica, the smallest province of the Audiencia de Guatemala, continued on its independent path, building its rural democracy and agriculturally based economy. With Spain's power waning and Costa Rica's de facto independence growing, there was little significant contact between the two over the years.

Independence
On September 15, 1821, when independence from Spain was declared by Guatemala for all of Central America, it actually had very little effect on the Costa Ricans. The settlers had long been accustomed to governing themselves, being basically ignored by their distant motherland. The news of the proclamation of independence actually took a month to reach Costa Rica from the seat of Spanish government in Guatemala City. A hastily convened provincial council in Costa Rica voted for accession to Mexico, which had declared independence earlier in the year. Then, in 1823, the other Central American countries proclaimed the United Provinces (Federation) of Central America, with Guatemala City as its capital. Costa Ricans

were divided between those who wanted to join the newly proclaimed Mexican Empire and those who favored the Federation based on Guatemala.

The conservative and aristocratic leaders of Cartago and Heredia were for the Empire, and the more liberal progressive leaders of San José and Alajuela were for the Central American Federation, or independence. These differences came to a head in 1823, resulting in a brief civil war. After a short struggle, San José and Alajuela were victorious, and San José was finally established as the capital in 1835. Costa Rica became part of the federal United Provinces of Central America—embracing El Salvador, Guatemala, Honduras, and Nicaragua—with full autonomy for its own affairs. The province of Guanacaste soon after seceded from Nicaragua to join the nation of Costa Rica.

Colonial institutions had been notoriously weak in Costa Rica. Modernization of the economy after independence helped to pull the population out of poverty and developed a firm foundation of democracy much earlier than elsewhere in the isthmus.

Liberalism and reform were the most important tools used to counter the social unrest caused by the rivalry between the conservatives of Cartago and Heredia and the liberals from San José and Alajuela. Juan Mora Fernández, a schoolteacher, was elected the first head of state by Congress in 1824. He is respected to this day for the establishment of a sound judicial system, the first newspaper, and expanding the reaches of public education. With much foresight, he sparked an enthusiasm in the cultivation of coffee and gave free land grants to farmers who would plant this valuable crop. Costa Rica seceded from the Federation and became a fully sovereign state in 1838.

There followed a period of effective dictatorship under Braulio Carrillo Colina, who was removed by General Francisco Morazán Queseda, a Honduran, who attempted to relaunch the regional federation. His overthrow led to a liberal enlightenment. A new constitution was introduced, and in 1848 the young president José María Castro Madriz formally declared Costa Rica a republic.

The following president, Juan Rafael Mora Porras, is famous for mobilizing a force of Costa Rican volunteers against the mercenary force of the North American adventurer William Walker. Walker was an incorrigible freebooter from the southern United States, with ambitions to conquer Central America and turn it into a slave state annexed to the USA. He may well be one of the reasons for the negative connotations given to the word *gringo,* and for the phrase "the ugly American." The famous battle at La Casona ranch in Guanacaste on March 20, 1856, lasted a mere fourteen minutes, with the Ticos victoriously ousting the *filibusteros*. They chased them back into Nicaragua, where in Rivas they clashed again on April 11, 1856. The young Alajuelan drummer boy Juan Santamaría became a national hero when

he volunteered to set fire to the wooden building where Walker's band had taken refuge. He was shot dead as he carried out the action, and is now honored for his bravery each April 11, Juan Santamaría Day. The episode was a defining moment for Costa Ricans, instilling in them a sense of national pride.

The "Grain of Gold"

First introduced from Cuba in the late eighteenth century, coffee soon became king, creating prosperity for the young country and power for the coffee barons, the *cafeteleros.* Profits from the coffee boom were spent on the country's infrastructure and other projects, and fueled the import of European fashions and ideas into Costa Rica. Rivalry between these wealthy families caused them to vie for political

power. In 1849 they ousted President José María Castro Madriz, replacing him with Juan Rafael Mora Porras, a prominent *cafetelero*. From 1840 to 1890 the economy was dependent upon the cash crop.

The struggle between the coffee barons and the military culminated in 1870 in a coup by General Tomás Guardia Gutiérrez. Although he was a military dictator, his twelve-year rule was in many ways benign. He ordered the construction of a railroad from the Central Valley to the Caribbean coast to facilitate the transport of coffee. The job was undertaken by the North American entrepreneur Minor Cooper Keith; it claimed the lives of more than five thousand laborers and was completed only in 1890. Workers were recruited from China, Italy, and then Jamaica. Keith was awarded vast tracts of land, among other benefits, for his services. He founded the United Fruit Company to cultivate bananas on these lands, laying the base for Costa Rica's prosperous banana industry. Many of the Jamaican railway workers ended up working on the banana plantations.

A Budding Democracy

In 1889 President Bernardo Soto Alfaro held the first "honest" election, with the full participation of the population, though excluding women and blacks. Much to his surprise his opponent won the day, and Soto decided not to recognize the new president. The people of Costa Rica rose up and marched in the streets to make their views known, and Soto was forced to step down. This event laid the foundations for the peaceful transfer of power and political stability that Costa Rica continues to enjoy.

Democracy once again faced a challenge in 1917, when the agricultural elites removed Alfredo Gonzalez Flores as president, replacing him with the Minister of War, Federico Tinoco Granados. Tinoco's iron rule outraged the people. The Ticos felt they had earned their liberty and rose up once again, with women and high-school students marching in the streets. In 1918 General Jorge Volio Jiménez led a coup against Tinoco, who fled the country. Jorge Volio founded the Reformist Party in 1923, which advocated social and agrarian reform. The 1930s saw the Great Depression, poverty, and social conflict, and the spread of both Fascist and Communist ideas. With the outbreak of war in Europe, the markets for bananas and coffee collapsed. Despite these problems, the government continued to invest in public health and education.

Liberal Reforms
The 1940s marked a turning point in Costa Rican history from the paternalistic rule of the agricultural elites to a modern urbanized state, with bureaucrats, professionals, and small entrepreneurs controlling the levers of power. The winner of the 1940 elections was Rafael Angel Calderón Guardia, a conservative, profoundly religious physician with a social conscience. His presidency is noted for wide-ranging social reform. He introduced workers' rights, a minimum wage, and paid vacations, and offered peasants the right to own wasteland that

they cultivated. He also created the University of Costa Rica and formed the *Partido Unidad Social Cristiana* (PUSC)—the United Christian Socialist Party. These reforms, however, alienated the propertied classes.

The effects of the Second World War and inflation stalled economic growth. Rising discontent saw Otilio Ulate Blanco, the candidate of the opposition *Partido Unión Nacional* (PUN)—the National Union Party—win the 1944 elections. The Congress refused to accept the result and simply replaced Calderón with a fellow Social Christian, Teodoro Picado, as president. Picado's uninspired rule failed to address popular concerns. Calderón ran for a second presidency in the elections of 1948, but Otilio Ulate Blanco won again. The *Calderonistas* called the elections fraudulent and Congress annulled the results, which plunged Costa Rica into a civil war on March 10, 1948.

The Civil War
José María Figueres Ferrer, known later as don Pépe, had been exiled to Mexico in 1942 by Calderón for his opposition to the government. While abroad he had made valuable alliances with other Central American countries. He returned in 1944, and when the elections of 1948 were annulled, he led a military uprising in defense of democracy.

Don Pépe's Army of National Liberation easily overcame Calderón and his poorly trained army in the forty-day war. His interim government introduced a new constitution that set out to redistribute power away from the elites and to

remove institutional corruption. Its landmark reforms included suffrage for women and full citizenship for Blacks. Probably his greatest accomplishment was the abolition of the army. Costa Rica is still respected today for not having an army. Don Pépe also nationalized the banks and insurance companies. Calderón and many of his followers were exiled to Mexico.

Once order had been restored, Figueres handed the reigns of power back to Otilio Ulate Blanco, the elected president, in 1949. Don Pépe went on to found the *Partido Liberación Nacional* (PLN)—the National Liberation Party. Opposition to the funding of public services by greater taxation of the rich now centered on the PUN.

Onward and Forward to the Present
The steady growth of social and economic progress through the years was accompanied by a peaceful exchange of power every four years, passing back and forth between the two major parties, the socialist PLN and the centrist PUSC. The 1950s and '60s saw the state intervene actively in economic affairs, funded by tax revenues from healthy banana and coffee exports. Agricultural expansion led to widespread deforestation. Meanwhile many small farmers, unable to compete with the advanced techniques of the larger estates, left the land for the

cities. The economic boom ended with the global recession triggered by the oil crisis of 1973.

Costa Ricans enjoyed a rising standard of living through these years. However, the creation of a welfare state ran up spending deficits that drained the national budget and brought on an economic crisis in 1980. Inflation of epidemic proportions, currency devaluation, decreases in the prices of coffee, sugar, and bananas, huge oil bills, and trade disruptions caused by the civil war in neighboring Nicaragua and El Salvador all added to the economic burden. Austerity measures imposed by the IMF and large international loans, designed to relieve the debt crisis, created a further burden of debt that still plagues Costa Rica today. US offers of aid were designed to draw the country into taking sides in the Nicaraguan conflict.

In 1986 the presidency passed to Oscar Arias Sánchez of the PLN, who proposed a peace plan for the troubled region. His efforts to resolve Central America's conflicts were rewarded with the Nobel Peace Prize in 1987. This prestigious award brought great pride to the Ticos and global recognition to this small nation in the Central American isthmus.

In the 1990s tourism overtook bananas as the country's largest industry, and high-tech companies started investing in Costa Rica. In 1990 Rafael Angel Calderón Fournier, the PUSC candidate, won the elections and was inaugurated president fifty years after his father. He introduced a series of austerity measures to help alleviate the pressures from the country's huge deficit and national debt repayments, while trying to maintain the standards of public service unique to Costa Rica in the region.

The 1993 campaign was noteworthy for bringing the first woman to such prominence. Margarita Peñon, then wife of Oscar Arias, ran for president, but the winner was the PLN candidate, José María Figueres Olsen, son of don Pépe. Clearly the history of Costa Rican politics has been strongly influenced by a handful of families. It was hard for Figueres to live up to the iconic stature of his father. He became an unpopular president. His campaign promises to improve health care and education were not fulfilled, thwarted by price hikes, tax increases, bank closures, and strikes by public employees. Efforts were made to diversify the economy, however, and Intel opened a microprocessor manufacturing plant in the central highlands in 1998.

Miguel Angel Rodríguez, on the PUSC ticket, won the 1998 elections. This campaign was notable for first-time occurrences: the first black candidate, and the first all-women ticket. Two presidential candidates had women in both vice-presidential positions, as well. Rodríguez won by a very slight percentage. His term was noted for an increase in tourism, the growth of high-tech products, which was a boost for the sagging economy, and a decline in the value of banana and coffee exports as commodity prices fell. His attempts to privatize state companies led to massive street demonstrations.

The elections in 2000 presented a choice between Abel Pacheco on the PUSC ticket, Rolando Araya on the PLN ticket, and a first-ever seriously accepted third contender, the Citizen Action Party (PAC). The PAC candidate, Otton Solís, ran on a strong platform against corruption and ineffectual government. The people of Costa Rica were ready for a change. The three-candidate race resulted in a run-off election between the top two candidates, for the first time since 1949. Abel Pacheco won with 58 percent of the vote, a victory attributed in part to his celebrity from his TV program. His time in office, however, was plagued by resignations of cabinet ministers, and lack of cohesiveness hampered his government's performance. The Central American Free Trade Agreement (CAFTA), known locally as TLC (*Trato de Libre Comercio*), generated great opposition, expressed in huge street demonstrations. There was a marked division among Ticos regarding its benefits. While big business considered it a necessity to enable them to compete in a global economy, many small farmers, businesses, and environmentalists saw it as their ruin. Eventually, in 2008, the government voted to join CAFTA.

In October 2004 the country was plagued by corruption scandals involving former high-ranking officials. Two ex-presidents, Miguel Angel Rodríguez and Rafael Angel Calderón, were tried, convicted, and jailed. Other officials of the CCSS, the state-run social security health system, and from ICE, the state-run electricity and telecommunications company, were also jailed and many others investigated for alleged corruption. José María Figueres, a third ex-president, and the son of don Pépe, was also investigated for allegedly accepting large "gifts" in return for awarding contracts. Now living in Switzerland, he refused to return home for seven years, until the statute of limitation for his alleged corruption had expired. Then, surprisingly, Figueres arrived in December 2011, causing a nationwide stir, from government authorities down to the humblest citizen. He traveled to several areas of the country campaigning for his party, the PLN.

Figueres returned again in January 2012 and appeared before the Legislative Assembly where he was questioned over the corruption charges. Apparently, rather than provide adequate answers to questions from the authorities, he delivered more of a dissertation on his innocence. Many remain dissatisfied with his refusal to answer questions about the scandal. It remains to be seen if he will return to campaign for the 2014 elections, possibly for president. Many people seem to have short memories and the Figueres name, highly respected because of his beloved father, don Pépe, may yet return.

THE REGIONS

History and geography have combined to unite the seven provinces of Costa Rica into a single, peaceful fraternity. Despite distinct regional differences, the Ticos share a strong sense of national identity. The seven provinces are Guanacaste, Puntarenas, Limón, Heredia, Alajuela, Cartago, and San José.

Guanacaste

The large northwestern province of Guanacaste once belonged to Nicaragua. Its secession is celebrated every year on July 25, the Annexation of Guanacaste. This province differs from the rest of the country in being strongly influenced by indigenous culture, and the mixture of peoples has given the *Guanacastecos* their rich *moreno* (dark brown) complexion. They maintain many of the Chorotegas' historical and cultural traditions—in their foods, dances, and local crafts—and the hot tropical region of Guanacaste is the source of many of the indigenous traditions still treasured and practiced nationally today. Their folklore and dances are widely valued as part of the national patrimony. The people of Guanacaste are known for their openness and spontaneity.

Liberia, the capital, is located along the Inter-American highway. Its airport has become an important entry point for tourists. Guanacaste is a land of natural beauty encompassing lowland "dry" forests, vast, windswept plains, impressive volcanic mountain ranges, cloud forest and rain forest, national parks with vast underground caves, and miles of spectacular tropical beaches along the Pacific coast.

The cowboys, or *sabaneros*, of the Guanacaste plains tend herds of cattle on large ranches, an occupation dating from the time when the region was still a part of Nicaragua. The cultivation of abundant and exquisite fruits, such as papaya, *guanabana*, and melons, is also an

important local industry. The tourism boom of the last few decades has brought a flourishing economy to the area.

Puntarenas

The long Pacific coastal lands of Puntarenas stretch from Guanacaste south to the border of Panama. This tropical land offers sandy beaches, small bays, hidden coves, and lowland rain forest. In the southern Pacific area, the Osa Peninsula is home to Corcovado National Park, famous for the incredible richness of its flora and fauna. The lowland areas around Golfito were once flourishing banana plantations. Fishing, for food and sport, continues to be an important industry. Ecotourism has created a sustainable way to create an economic gain from the beautiful natural resources, while at the same time protecting them.

The city of Puntarenas, the capital of the province, is a major port. The frequent arrival of cruise ships, docking there for the day, has given tourism in the area a new dimension. Puntarenas is the departure point for exploring the Nicoya Peninsula on ferries, which transport both vehicles and people. *Puntarenenses* are fun-loving and laid-back, and take full advantage of their paradisiacal land.

Limón

The province of Limón extends along Costa Rica's Caribbean coast. Its colorful culture reflects a rich mixture of people of Afro-Caribbean, indigenous Indian, Spanish, and Chinese descent. Afro-Caribbeans from Jamaica were brought to the area to work on the railroad that facilitated the transport of coffee from San José to the port of Limón. They are the predominant community, and they continue to speak English as well as Spanish. The indigenous cultures have managed to preserve several of their native languages. The humid tropical climate produces flourishing banana and cacao plantations. Coconut production continues to be important to the locals.

In the northeastern area, trips along the Tortuguero canals reveal abundant wildlife and lush, verdant jungles. In an effort to increase economic productivity by making the waterways navigable, the rivers and lagoons were dredged and interconnected with an artificial canal system, officially opened in 1974. The canals are now a major attraction for tourists, naturalists, and anglers. Many hardwoods in the area were saved at the same time by the creation of national parks. Turtle-nesting areas on the coast near

Tortuguero are protected, and the large sea turtles draw many tourists to the area.

Puerto Limón is an important port and the capital of the province. Cruise ships boost the local economy when they dock there for the day. The city's historical architecture is charming, with its typical Caribbean influence, characterized by two-story wooden houses with large balconies. The city is sorely in need of renovation, a source of discontent for the people, who feel they are ignored by the central government.

For a glimpse of local culture, go to the palm-filled Central Park, Parque Vargas, and the Central Market. In this hot and humid area, life is lived outdoors, and you can learn much by just observing. In October there is a spectacular *carnaval*, celebrating the arrival of Columbus, now called *Día de las Razas*. Bands, dancers, singers, and spectators alike join in the festivities. Typical Afro-Caribbean food features rice and beans cooked in coconut oil and other delicacies, such as *rondón* (fish and vegetable stew), *patí* (meat and vegetable patty), and *pan bon* (rum-spiked fruitcake).

Cahuita and Puerto Viejo to the south of Limón offer long expanses of secluded beaches. In the south the Bribri indigenous community near the Panamanian border offers a glimpse into the past. With its unique Caribbean culture, this area offers an experience not to be found in otherparts of Costa Rica.

Limonenses of all backgrounds have united in their struggle with the government for equality and more financial investment in the area. They feel their geographically isolated region has been overlooked for years. Recently a contract for a new million dollar container port in Moin was approved. The new terminal aims to reduce unloading and loading time from five days to a single day. It will also significantly raise the nation's ranking in port services. About 75–80 percent of the country's goods pass through

the port of Moin. In addition, the Refinadora Costarricense de Petroleo and the China National Petroleum Corporation have launched a joint venture to build a US $96 million facility to handle tankers nearby. This new investment on the Caribbean coast is a welcome boost for Limón.

San José

The province of San José is situated in the heart of the country. The city of San José is the capital. *Josefinos* are proud of their modern, cosmopolitan city, and the history that created it. Many Ticos are drawn to it, looking for a better life. The people are more sophisticated—and more punctual—than other Ticos, and work hard to maintain their position and job security in an age of fierce competition for jobs and education. Business interactions with foreigners have helped to make the *Josefinos* a competing force in the global economy.

The temperate climate has been called perfect, and is another reason this area has drawn so many people to the city and surrounding foothills. While the city is the center of national business, economic, and political affairs, the outlying reaches of the province produce rich harvests of coffee, sugarcane, fruits, vegetables, and flowers. The University of Costa Rica, located in San Pedro de Montes de Oca, provides a rich opportunity for higher education to the interested public who can meet the competitive entrance requirements. San José is the central hub for communication with the other provinces, with road systems and air routes leading into and out of the capital.

Heredia

Heredia, the smallest of the provinces, is home to the *Heredianos.* The capital city, Heredia, known as City of Flowers, has traditionally been conservative. This dates back to colonial times, when the conservative aristocratic families of Cartago and Heredia were vying for political power with the more progressive residents of Alajuela and San José. Heredia's coffee barons have long reaped the benefits of their investment in the golden bean, which has brought prosperity to this rich, high-altitude, coffee-growing area.

The northern region of Heredia extends to the Nicaraguan border, through an area of humid

lowlands and rushing rivers that flow into the San Juan River, which separates Costa Rica and Nicaragua. The mountains surrounding the city of Heredia are covered with cloud and rain forests, inviting visitors to explore the trails through the national park on the Barva volcano. Heredia is the birthplace of Manuel María Gutiérrez, the inspirational author of the national anthem, and a source of pride to its citizens. It is home to the National University (UNA). The past decade has brought an enormous influx of foreign students who have come to study at the UNA, adding new diversity to the makeup of the city. The Central Park, Central Market, La Inmaculada Church, and the *Fortín* (Little Fort) are all testimony to the area's rich historical roots. Like so many cities in the country, the combination of past and present in Heredia creates a varied and interesting setting.

Alajuela

Alajuela is the proud homeland of Costa Rica's national hero, Juan Santamaría. The *Alajuelenses* tend to be more laid-back than the other people of the Central Valley. The city of Alajuela, the capital of the province, is 3,100 feet (945 meters) above sea level, and has a slightly warmer climate than the rest of the central highlands, which contributes to its more relaxed mode of life. The Central Park in

this city of mangoes is where *Alajuelenses* like to gather to share local gossip, spiced with their characteristic sly humor.

The farmers in the outlying areas produce rich crops of sugarcane and coffee. The canes are crushed in machines to extract the juice, to make *dulce,* an unrefined sugar, and *guaro*, a sugarcane liquor. The fertile valleys of San Carlos, in the northern zone, provide pasture for herds of cattle whose beef is both sold nationally and exported. In the surrounding foothills, dairy cows produce milk for a variety of dairy products. Beautiful forests of native hardwood trees cover the hillsides amid a network of rushing rivers. The live Arenal volcano in the northwest of the province is a spectacular sight, and is surrounded by thermal springs.

The Poás volcano that looms over the central valley has one of the world's widest craters. The forest around it is the habitat of tree ferns and gigantic *sombrilla del pobre*—"poor man's umbrella" plants. Alajuela is home to the Juan Santamaría International Airport, a connection with the wider world that reflects the progressive thinking instinctive to the *Alajuelenses.*

Cartago

Thanks to its healthy climate and fertile, volcanic soil, the province of Cartago, in the central highlands, was home to Costa Rica's first capital. As we have seen, Juan Vásquez de Coronado founded the city of Cartago in 1562, and was later appointed mayor by the King in recognition of his successful settlement of the city. On a trip to Spain soon thereafter, his ship sank, and he and his crew perished. The Costa Ricans lamented the loss of their benevolent *conquistador*. It is thought that their feelings of brotherhood and their peaceful nature are the legacy of this esteemed man.

The agreeable city of Cartago attracts many to the Basílica de Nuestra Señora de Los Angeles, dedicated to the patron saint of the nation. Every August believers make the pilgrimage to Cartago to honor their saint.

The ruins of an old colonial church, destroyed by earthquakes, now serve as a focal point in a park. In 1960 the towering Irazú volcano on the outskirts of the city erupted, causing floods and

destruction. Its slopes are now woven with picturesque vegetable, flower, and dairy farms that produce bountiful harvests. Cartago remains the cradle of the founding fathers of the nation.

THE CAPITAL, SAN JOSÉ

The Central Valley is the geographical, political, and economic heartland of Costa Rica, and home to its most important cities, with San José at the center.

San José, the capital of the nation, is situated at an altitude of 3,691 feet (1,125 meters) and is known for its perfect climate. It is home to nearly one-third of the country's population. Founded in 1737, it became the capital in 1823. San José was the third city in the world to have public electric lighting—an example of its progressive nature. This cosmopolitan city is characterized by a juxtaposition of modern and colonial architecture, and bustling streets. Earthquakes over the years have destroyed many of the colonial buildings, though some fine examples remain. The city is small enough to cover on foot, and walking is an intelligent option to beat the gridlocked traffic. The roads are divided into streets (*calles*) and avenues (*avenidas*), and laid out in a grid pattern.

San José's architectural gem is the National Theater, opened in 1897. This neoclassical structure was modeled on the Paris Grand Opera House, and has wonderful acoustics. The national symphony orchestra performs there, as well as an impressive variety of international artists. The coffee barons funded its construction in the era

when coffee was the true gold of the nation, and the Costa Ricans are proud of their national treasure. Barrio Amon is a residential area with some domestic architectural jewels. Several of these elegant old homes have been preserved as hotels.

The central market offers a little of everything, from fresh fruits and vegetables, herbs, and cut flowers, to clothes, kitchenware, and toys, as well as being a good place to mingle with the local crowd and enjoy a typical *casado* (rice, beans, cooked vegetable, and salad) at one of the numerous lunch counters.

Art galleries, museums, and theaters offer a wide choice of cultural activities. Conferences, discussions, and book and poetry readings are frequently held at various theaters, cultural centers, and embassies. Simply people watching, in the Central Park or Plaza de la Cultura, is a great way to relax and learn about the Ticos. La Sabana park, made on the site of the former city airport in the 1950s, is now a sprawling oasis of trees and grass. This is a popular weekend destination for *Josefinos*, where they can relax and enjoy the outdoors with their families. The old airport building on the east side of the park is now the Museum of Costa Rican Art. The city's criminal element is busy twenty-four hours a day here, so be vigilant, just as any Tico would.

GOVERNMENT
Costa Rica is a constitutional democracy with a unicameral Legislative Assembly, which is elected directly every four years. The elections of 2006 returned Oscar Arias Sánchez of the PLN as president. In the 2010 elections his vice president and justice minister, Laura Chinchilla, became

Costa Rica's first female president. Costa Ricans are proud of their democracy. On turning eighteen everyone has the right to vote. Ticos consider it a duty to use this privilege, and the result is an extremely high voter turnout. The citizens actively want to participate.

Laura Chinchilla ran on an anti-crime and pro-trade platform. She is a social conservative, opposing gay marriage and abortion. She has been successful in promoting programs to support the elderly and infant day care centers, and has banned open pit mining and closed down a very controversial Canadian gold mining project in Las Crucitas, near the Nicaraguan border. This was seen as a major success for environmentalists both in Costa Rica and Nicaragua.

However, a UNIMER poll in January 2012 showed that 90 percent of Costa Ricans did not believe she exercised effective control in the country, and that government agencies were riddled with corruption.

The distribution of power is divided among the executive, legislative, and judicial branches of government, in principle creating an efficient system of checks and balances. The executive is made up of the president and two vice presidents, as well as the nineteen cabinet ministers, selected by the president. The legislature is made up of fifty-seven deputies who are elected every four years to represent the seven provinces. Population determines the number of deputies for each province. The judiciary is made up of the Supreme Court, divided into four chambers, with twenty-two magistrates chosen by the Legislative Assembly. The Sala IV, or Constitutional Chamber, decides on court cases involving constitutional issues. It is famous for upholding the constitutional rights of the common people.

The Political Constitution was enacted in 1949. Later, a powerful independent body, the Supreme Electoral Tribunal (TSE), was created by an amendment to the constitution to oversee elections. In 1969 an amendment limited the president to one term of office, without the possibility of reelection. In 2003 the Sala IV overturned this law, making reelection possible, and the popular ex-president Oscar Arias was eligible to run again and win by a narrow margin.

Throughout its history, Costa Rica has cultivated the development of democracy and emphasized human rights. This tendency toward greater democracy and equality stands out in a region plagued by social and political unrest. Enlightened political leaders, comparative prosperity, and educational opportunity that has created a stable middle class, are all factors that sustain the democratic ideal. Having abolished the military, the country has avoided the kinds of political intervention by the army that are so common in neighboring countries. Costa Rica maintains only domestic police and security forces for internal security.

The recent scandals, involving three former presidents from both of the main parties and high-ranking officials of the state-run social security system and electricity and telecommunications company, have led to the creation of several new independent parties. The results of the 2014 presidential elections are bound to bring about interesting changes to Costa Rican politics

THE ECONOMY

Costa Rica's economy has slowly changed over the years from being totally based on agriculture to today's mixture of tourism, component production for the high-tech industry, high-tech support call centers, exports such as flowers and ornamental plants, and the traditional cultivation of bananas, pineapples, and coffee

Tourism now brings in more foreign exchange than bananas and coffee combined, as Costa Rica's extraordinary biodiversity makes it a key ecotourism destination. The 2012 Environmental Performance Index (EPI) by Yale and Columbia universities ranks

Costa Rica as the fifth greenest country in the world—great news for the ecotourism industry.

Before the global economic crisis of 2009, Costa Rica enjoyed steady economic growth. Tourism took a big dive in the recession, as did construction and real estate. Its moderate fragile recovery is only now being felt. The economy contracted in 2009 but resumed growth at about 4 percent a year in 2010–11.

Foreign investors remain attracted by the country's political stability and relatively high education levels, as well as the incentives offered in the free-trade zones. Since coming into force on January 1, 2009, the Central American Free Trade Agreement has increased foreign direct investment in key economic sectors, including insurance and telecommunications. However, business still suffers from high levels of bureaucracy, legal uncertainty due to overlapping and sometimes conflicting responsibilities between agencies, the difficulty of enforcing contracts, and weak investor protection.

Interestingly, in the last few years China has become a welcome investor in the country. The Chinese funded and constructed a new national soccer stadium in San José, completely built by Chinese workers. This new jewel was inaugurated in early 2011 and has become a popular venue for soccer games, concerts, and festivals.

China is also funding, together with the municipality, the construction of a Chinatown, *Barrio Chino*, in San José. This new attraction, which includes a 1,969 foot (600 meter) pedestrian-only boulevard lit by Chinese-style lamps, is intended to promote more foreign tourism in the capital.

China, Mexico, and Costa Rica form a matrix of manufacturing centers of high quality technical products for many transnational companies. Costa Rica's geographical position makes it well suited to be a center of distribution for the area.

Despite the mild recuperation, the economy remains delicately dependent on the international situation and the price of oil. Growing pains continue, as does urbanization, which reached 64 percent in 2010. Poverty is around 15–20 percent, and the social safety net that had been put in place by the government has been eroded by financial constraints on government expenditure, giving rise to social strains.

A growing number of college graduates are facing fierce competition for jobs. The Occupy Movement made its presence felt in San José in October 2011. About three hundred protestors rallied for social justice and against corporate greed and failing economic policies. This was referred to locally as the "*Movimiento de los Indignados*" (movement of the outraged).

VALUES &
ATTITUDES

Although no prototypical Tico exists in reality, by and large Costa Ricans tend to share broadly liberal values and attitudes. They are known for their friendliness, helpfulness, and hospitality, and have a healthy curiosity, which allows them to accept the possibility of valid alternatives. They judge for themselves whether "different" is positive or negative.

Costa Rica is an island of relative stability in an area of political and social unrest. Broad social welfare policies have created a self-assured people who live in relative comfort. Ticos tend to look for compromise and peaceful resolutions, though when their rights are challenged they have no qualms about protesting. With a literacy rate of 96 percent and electricity and phone service available to 95 percent of the population, the Ticos appear to be generally content with their lot.

For the visitor, lack of punctuality is another, less endearing, trait found in Costa Rica, as it is in so many Latin countries. People living in warmer climates appear to have a more relaxed interpretation of time. Accepting this difference can avoid frustration.

Socializing—whether family gatherings or getting together with friends or business associates—is an important part of life in Costa Rica. Ticos are used to living, working, and playing together, and have developed habits of tolerance and cooperation. The solidarity of working together for the well-being of the whole is a Tico characteristic. Making the best of a situation and adapting has proved helpful in their society, and is a good example for visitors.

FAMILY VALUES

Costa Rica is a strongly family-oriented society. If anything is sacred, it is the family. Children are seen and heard everywhere, and treated with loving care by everyone.

It is quite common for the older generation to live with their children and grandchildren. They are an integral part of the family, and add in many ways to the smooth running and good atmosphere of the household. The grandmother often prepares meals and looks after the children when the parents are at work, and the grandparent–grandchild relationship is a strong bond.

In the past, families tended to live in the same areas throughout their lives. This phenomenon has changed with the movement of people for study and jobs, but the strong ties remain. Since Costa Rica is so small, to visit someone on the other side of the country is probably only a few hours' drive.

Despite the availability of contraceptives, large numbers of children continue to be born from unplanned pregnancies. Abortion is not officially legal in Costa Rica and the Catholic Church frowns on the idea of a realistic sexual education program in public schools. Teen pregnancies out of wedlock continue to confront society, though generally Costa Ricans see and accept all children as a blessing. Family gatherings form an important support system.

With the growing number of single-mother households, Costa Rica's family makeup has become more diverse. Families with a single mother have become even more numerous than those with both father and mother. No matter who makes up the group, however, family ties are strong. The woman traditionally runs the household, and today's women are facing the challenge of full-time employment as well. With more girls progressing to further education than in the past, women today have more options in the world of work, and there is a growing number of professional women in highly respected positions.

Ticos thoroughly enjoy celebrating. Whether it is a wedding, birthday, graduation, baby shower, funeral, or other important event, they unite to express their support and wishes for the family.

The Matriarch

Doña María, aged sixty-seven, is the mother of eight children, ranging from fifty to twenty-seven years old. Though she has never had a husband or a man of the house, she has always been greatly respected in her small, rural community. She labored many years as a domestic worker, and raised a family of healthy, hardworking children. She now enjoys staying at home caring for her grandchildren, while her children are an integral part of the local workforce.

RESPECT FOR ELDERS

Traditionally, Costa Ricans respect and care for their elders. This attitude prevails today despite the social changes through the years, which have led to differences in how the care is provided. Today, as a result of social and economic changes, there is a more open acceptance of elder care outside the family. An increase in the number of elder care homes in the last decade has made this option more popular. It is also now acceptable for healthy older individuals to live alone. People generally respect the wisdom of older people, which has been learned through the years and is given with love. Talking with older Costa Ricans can be a fascinating way to learn about the past and how it has influenced today's culture.

Elders who turn sixty-five are awarded the privilege of a gold card issued by the government, which is valid for discounts or free passage on buses and reduced-price entrances to many places. Elderly people are given the priority of a seat on a bus and to be the first in line.

HOSPITALITY

Costa Ricans are very friendly, and enjoy getting to know their foreign visitors. They are both curious and helpful, and will do their best to make you feel at home. It would not be unusual for them to invite you to their home, after you have become acquainted. This is especially true in the *campo*, or rural areas, where life is more informal than in the cities. Take advantage of the opportunity to get firsthand experience of a hospitable Costa Rican home. Food will be offered—anything from a full meal to a *cafecito* (coffee) and a savory or sweet snack. This is one of the best ways to become acquainted with the Ticos, and they will enjoy the interaction as much as you will. Also, as English fluency is in great demand, they are always happy to find an opportunity to practice.

RELIGION

Costa Rica is officially a Roman Catholic country, though freedom of religion is guaranteed by the constitution, and tolerance prevails because it is believed that one has the right to honor God in one's own way.

While those of the older generation are regular churchgoers, for younger people this is confined to the celebrations of marriage, communion, and funerals, rather than weekly mass. In the last few years, scandals of sexual molestation by priests have led to calls for greater scrutiny and damaged the standing of the Church. There is a pull away from traditional religious practice, and Christian sects, especially Evangelical and fundamentalist groups, seem to be increasing in popularity. The majority of the people, however, are firmly Roman Catholic. There is also a stable Jewish community, with European roots. Jewish Ticos are well represented in the national business world and in the government.

The use of saints' names for towns, housing estates, and schools is widespread. People make frequent references to God in their everyday talk, for example, "*Si Dios quiere*," "God willing," or "*Vaya con Dios*," "Go with God." Religion appears to be more of a tradition than a practice.

There is no separation of Church and state in Costa Rica. Catholicism is taught as a subject in all public schools, though students may be exempted from the class if a waiver is signed on the grounds of different religious beliefs.

TOLERANCE AND PREJUDICE

Ticos tend to be pretty tolerant people. They take the daily long lines and time-consuming bureaucracy in their stride with patience and acceptance. They are tolerant of the unknown, unless it proves to be threatening.

Although racial prejudice is not apparent in today's society, it was definitely an issue in the past. The Black Afro-Caribbeans who had settled on the Atlantic coast after being brought to Costa Rica to work on the railroad were prohibited from entering the Central Valley for many years. In 1949 Blacks finally gained full citizenship, along with women's suffrage, and were allowed to integrate fully into Costa Rican society. Today's social hierarchy is based more on economics than race. People of all ethnic backgrounds compete for powerful positions in business and the government.

The recent immigration of large numbers of Nicaraguans and Colombians has raised a few eyebrows. Costa Ricans are concerned about immigrants taking advantage of the nation's social programs, thereby straining the economy. Tolerance generally prevails, however, probably due to the basic comfortable lifestyle of the majority of Ticos.

The Costa Rican media appears to be tolerant of violence in movies and on TV, in its newscasts and programs, though all are rated for public viewing. There is one national station that is dedicated to nonviolent broadcasting.

PRIDE, HONOR, AND *MACHISMO*

Costa Ricans are proud of their beautiful country and its stable democracy. They delight in showing visitors their national treasures. The contentedness of the growing middle class with the opportunities open to them is evident. The only area where self-respect appears to be lacking is in the general disregard for the cleanliness of public areas—streets, beaches, and sidewalks. This litter problem is apparent to most visitors. It is a mystery why people who are so conscious of their personal appearance and their tidy homes should feel free to discard their trash so casually.

National honor took a brutal beating during the last months of 2004, with the incarceration of two ex-presidents and high-ranking government officials. Many Ticos are deeply saddened and hurt by the corruption of these officials. The scandal has hurt Costa Rica's public image globally, and they feel

their honor has been impugned. Justice served will
help to boost the honor of the nation both nationally
and internationally.

Machismo—the best simile for this would be
"male chauvinism"—still exists. *Machismo* has a
long tradition in Latin cultures, and though still
encountered today, it is being challenged.
Changes in society—the large percentage of
women in the workplace and heading

Overcoming Machismo

Xiomara, a forty-year-old Costa Rican dentist,
was looking for a vacation home out in the
country, away from the hustle and bustle of the
city where she lives and works. On the rural slope
of the Turrialba volcano she found just what she
was looking for. The owner of the house, an
elderly man, was pleased to show her the
property, but when Xiomara wanted to negotiate
the purchase, he asked her to fetch her husband.
Xiomara responded that she wasn't married.
"Then bring your father or brother," insisted the
old man. Xiomara explained that her father had
passed away and that she didn't have a brother.
Only after a great deal of further discussion did
the old man finally decide that it would be
acceptable to negotiate the sale with a woman—
and eventually she became the happy owner of
the house!

households, and the general globalization of society—have all had an impact on this syndrome. Costa Rica appears to be on the right track, but it will be a while before it sees the end of *machismo*.

MANNERS

Costa Rica is definitely a "please and thank you" society. It's regarded as common courtesy to use these magic words. For example, on alighting from a bus many people thank the driver. Costa Ricans are polite, and expect politeness in return.

A traditional formality often accompanies a first encounter, especially with the older generation. For instance, you might use the *Usted* form of address, which shows more respect than the informal pronoun *tu*. Once you've been introduced, formalities quickly fade away and a genuine friendly interaction is common. For example, when first introduced, the title of *Señor* or *don* would be added to a man's name—*Señor Alvaro Ramirez* or *don Alvaro*—but these titles are dropped once there is a more friendly relationship. Acquaintances usually greet each other with a kiss on the cheek if it is two women or a man and a woman. Men usually shake hands unless they know each other well, when a hug is the norm.

It is customary to offer your seat to an elderly or disabled person, a pregnant woman, or one holding a small child. These people are given priority, going straight to the front of the line in banks, public services, or just about anywhere.

Extreme Manners

Guido, the local high-school English teacher in a small rural community, invited a North American family to dine at his house, by way of thanks for their help with his English. The guests accepted the invitation with pleasure, and duly arrived. To their surprise they were seated at the table and served, while Guido and his family stood watching them respectfully as they ate. It was a totally new experience for them not to have their hosts sit down and share the meal with them.

Normally compliments are plentiful. Costa Rican males traditionally express their appreciation of a female passerby. Such a *piropo* should not be seen as an insult, because that is not the intention. It is just a different way of behaving in a *macho* society. Men often call women *guapa*, *princesa*, or *reina*. Some visitors take offense at these apparently degrading comments. If you just ignore the remark, it will end there. This is not considered a rude custom, so do accept it for the compliment it is intended to be.

MAÑANA

The *mañana* syndrome is alive and well in Costa Rica. This common Latin quality of "putting-off-until-later" can be quite disconcerting to foreigners with a strict "just-do-it" philosophy. Literally, *mañana* can be translated as either "tomorrow" or "morning," but the real meaning in this circumstance is "later" or "much later." Don't expect something to be done tomorrow just because it was put off today. In general, things seem to take much longer than anticipated.

Another similar and commonly used word is *ahora,* or *ahorita.* Although this is translated as "now," or "right now," it actually means "later," or "a little later." Ticos often like to leave fate in the hands of God. "*Si Dios quiere*" ("God willing") is commonly heard, as in, for example, "*Si Dios quiere,* I'll see you tomorrow at noon." If you are in a situation where something really needs to be done immediately, however, just take the time to explain the urgency, and insist on it.

BEATING THE SYSTEM

The rising cost of living, the devaluation of the *colon,* and salaries that make it hard to make ends meet all contribute to the pervasive attitude of trying to beat the system. If you can bend the rules a bit here or there to your benefit, so be it. Just don't get caught.

Bribes, *chorizos,* are common, though they are officially frowned upon. If someone is pulled over for a traffic infraction he may ask the officer if he can "treat him to lunch" or "help him out" rather than get a ticket. Since the officer's salary is meager, he may well cooperate, thereby making a little extra for himself.

Growing-Up Fast

Ronald learned his first hands-on lesson about beating the system at fourteen years old. He was driving his go-cart down the road to his friend's house at the corner when he was spotted by a traffic policeman, who asked to see his license. Neither boy nor go-cart was licensed. The policeman said he wanted to talk to Ronald's father, and accompanied him home. The policeman explained to father and son that as well as paying the fine for driving without a license, if one received a ticket for driving under age before obtaining a license, it made it difficult to obtain one when one came of age. He suggested that he could "help them out" if they "bought him lunch." The father turned to his son and said, "This is part of learning to drive—you handle it." Ronald and the policeman quickly negotiated the price of lunch. Ronald paid him the equivalent of US $5, and the policeman contentedly gave Ronald the right, even though it was still illegal, to ride his go-cart on the side street only.

Paying someone else to do the running around or hold a place in a line for you will often simplify matters and bypass time-consuming red tape when dealing with the bureaucracy. Any way you can get around the system without causing undue attention is acceptable.

The recent incarceration of past presidents and high-ranking officials has left ordinary Costa Ricans feeling cheated. Corrupt officials who customarily line their pockets with public funds enrage the citizens, so Ticos feel entitled to get as much out of the system as possible. They want the system to work for them, but when it throws up obstacles they are inclined to take things into their own hands.

ATTITUDES TOWARD FOREIGNERS

Increasing globalization has created an international blend of people and cultures in Costa Rica. In the Central Valley there are numerous foreign students studying at the universities and at language schools. The boom in tourism has also made foreigners a common sight in the country. A large population of foreign residents can be found in many areas.

The prevalent attitude toward foreigners is one of acceptance and curiosity. Ticos welcome them for opening up new opportunities, and possibly new jobs. Many people see the foreigners' money bringing benefits to the country, and feel they should treat their guests with hospitality and respect. There is the occasional person who will try to take advantage of a foreigner, and there are of course outright criminals who see foreigners as an easy target for theft.

The immigration of many Nicaraguans and Colombians in the last few years has put a strain on the economy, and many Costa Ricans have negative feelings toward them because of this. *Nicas* have unfortunately become stigmatized as thieves. Those who come to Costa Rica are from the poorest classes and take the lowest-paid jobs. Colombian immigrants are often unfairly thought to be involved with drugs or some kind of black market trade. Most Colombians who come here are from the middle class.

Gringos, North Americans from the United States, can also cause resentment, though most of the distrust is focused on the US government and its policies rather than the citizens.

TICO DIRECTIONS
Ticos like to be helpful, but if you have lost your way the directions they give can be confusing or annoying for visitors. The words north, south, east, and west are commonly used, so learn to tune into the sun, or carry a compass! Few streets and avenues have signs, so a Tico may tell you that you need to go, "Three hundred meters north of El Mercadito store." An added challenge is created when a landmark that no longer exists is used as a point of reference—"A hundred meters west of the old school house." If you lived

locally you would know where the old school house was, but you are a visitor, and don't.

A further challenge confronts those seeking directions. Many people wanting to be helpful may not really know what you are asking for, but still try to help, rather than tell you they don't know. It's a good idea to get several opinions to make sure you are headed in the right direction. Remember that the Ticos' intentions are positive—they really are trying to help.

chapter three

CUSTOMS *&*
TRADITIONS

Costa Rica is rich in local customs and traditions, and celebration of their national heritage is an integral part of Tico culture. From an early age children in school learn dances, songs, and reenactments of historical events to celebrate important holidays. The influx of foreigners into the country and the cultural threat from globalization have actually prompted a revival of enthusiasm for customs and traditions as a way of preserving national identity. Although the majority of these customs have religious origins, the actual practice has more social significance. A few holidays commemorate purely historical events.

It is often mandatory for children to attend school on a national holiday to participate in an *acto cívico*, or civic act, for a few hours. The celebration of these holidays is always a good excuse for a party. Whether it is a small town's local saint's day or a nationwide holiday, joining in a *fiesta* is a wonderful way to become immersed into Tico culture.

PUBLIC HOLIDAYS

Not long ago, public holidays accounted for a constant stream of days off. Recently, to help create a more efficient work calendar, the number of public holidays was trimmed. Today, if a holiday falls on a weekend it is not moved. Many people take their annual vacation between Christmas and New Year, when many businesses close down. Holy Week is another popular vacation time, many people heading to the beach or mountains, and many places closing for Holy Thursday and Good Friday. There is a two-week school vacation in July, *vacación de quince días*, which is another popular time for a vacation.

NATIONAL HOLIDAYS

January 1: New Year's Day

March/April: Holy Thursday

March/April: Good Friday

April 11: Juan Santamaría Day (day of the national hero)

May 1: Labor Day

July 25: Annexation of Guanacaste

August 2: *La Virgen de Los Angeles*

August 15: Mother's Day

September 15: Independence Day

October 12: Day of Culture

December 25: Christmas Day

THE FESTIVAL CALENDAR

While some of the public holidays are basically just a day off, there are a few that are traditionally celebrated with days of partying. Joining in these festivities can be a memorable cultural experience. Here are some of the most outstanding:

Christmas (*Navidad*)

While December 25 is listed as the official holiday, any Tico will confirm that Christmas celebrations last the entire month of December. On the first day of December, the daily *La Nacion* declares "*Ya llegó la Navidad*," "Christmas has arrived," so be ready to *montarse la carreta*, or jump on the oxcart, and join in the celebration.

Costa Ricans receive an *aguinaldo* in December, which is an extra month's salary. This bonus is definitely an aid to the celebrations. Many Ticos take full advantage of it to buy new clothes for the family, appliances for the home, toys for the children, or whatever else is needed. Certainly the *aguinaldo* is long spent by the time the Christmas holidays come to a close.

The first weekend in December is the annual *Teletón*, which is a continual twenty-four hours of televised entertainment, mostly singers, on all the national TV channels. It is held to raise money for the Children's Hospital, with individuals and companies calling in day and night to make pledges, and is always a huge success. Children are deeply loved by Costa Ricans, so helping out the Children's Hospital is a popular choice.

La Festival de la Luz, usually the following weekend, is a colorful parade of floats with sparkling lights, marching bands, cheerleaders, and national celebrities. This event is held at night and is one of the most eagerly awaited festivals of the year. Families line the streets of San José to enjoy the spectacle. In 2004 the attendance was one million—a quarter of the population. Although this festival is relatively new, it appears to be here to stay.

Another tradition typical of the season is the *avenidazo*, held on the pedestrian mall of Avenida Central in San José. Between 6:00 and 9:00 p.m, people throw confetti at those walking along the avenue. The idea is to create an illusion of snow falling, with the confetti drifting through the air. There are free concerts in the avenue.

Las Posadas are the reenactment of the journey of Mary and Joseph. The children go from house to house singing *villancicos*, Christmas carols. This tradition appears to be making a comeback as Ticos realize the importance of holding on to their heritage.

A *portal*, or nativity scene, is traditional in homes at this time of year, as well as in churches, banks, and many public buildings. The *portal* in homes consists of Mary, Joseph, the three Kings, shepherds, and some animals, usually surrounded by dried moss, plants, shells, rocks, and painted background scenes. Family members add touches of their own, and it's not unusual to see toy cars, dolls, and plastic superheroes in the *portal*. The baby Jesus figure is laid into the crib on December 24. A *portal* can be small enough to fit on a tabletop, or large enough to fill an entire living room or front yard, with life-sized statues. This is a tradition where people excel in displaying their creativity.

Misa del Gallo is the Christmas Eve mass attended by many Catholics. Though traditionally celebrated at midnight, today many churches celebrate the mass at 9:00 p.m. or another convenient hour. *Nochebuena*, Christmas Eve, is usually the time for exchanging gifts, and the family enjoys a meal together.

December 25, Christmas Day, is celebrated with a family meal. The typical Christmas meal is *tamales*, a rich mixture of corn dough with vegetables and meat, wrapped in banana leaves and boiled. Families, especially those in the country, make hundreds of them for Christmas, and to offer their extended families and friends. Slaughtering a pig for the *tamales* is also a country tradition. Every cook has a special secret to make her *tamales* unique. Whenever anyone is hungry or visitors drop by, it's easy to heat up some *tamales*, and children and teenagers often compete to see how many they can eat. The hours of preparation pay off, as everyone enjoys the rich homemade creations, which often last a week or so. *Rompope,* or eggnog, is the drink of the season, while imported apples and grapes are special fruit treats, which can be bought at little stalls set up throughout the towns during this time of year. Christmas Day is as much a social occasion as a religious ceremony.

A few decades ago, it was the common belief that the *niño Jesús,* baby Jesus, brought children gifts for Christmas. Nowadays, with the influx of foreign traditions, Santa Claus and Christmas trees abound. Commercialization of the season is also rampant, with retailers enticing customers to buy, buy, buy.

December 26 is *El Tope*, the horse parade, in San José, with hundreds of brightly ornamented horses and riders prancing through the streets to the cheers of the crowds.

Bullfighting is also a part of the end-of-year *fiestas* celebrated in Zapote. In Costa Rica the bull is never killed or speared, and the public can enter the stadium to try their luck at fighting or teasing the bull. The spectators enjoy the confrontation between man and bull, and show their support with shouts of enthusiasm.

December 28 is the *Día de los Inocentes*, Costa Rica's April Fool's Day, when even national newspapers carry false stories to create a stir.

The Christmas season ends with the *rezo del niño* (prayer to the baby Jesus), any time after January 6, when the wise men arrive with their gifts for the child. Family and friends gather to say the rosary aloud together, sing of the birth of Jesus, and pray. Then it is time for refreshments.

Easter
The Easter celebration begins with Palm Sunday, the first day of *Semana Santa,* Holy Week. Large, impressive, artistic designs of colored sawdust are created in the streets, and the week is filled with elaborate dramatic street processions enacting the passion and crucifixion of Christ. Actors depicting Pontius Pilate, Jesus, Mary, and other biblical figures move through the streets, followed by the faithful fervently praying, and observers. On Holy Thursday and Good Friday the country virtually shuts down, including bus services and liquor sales. *Semana Santa* is celebrated as a time of reflection and rest. Several towns are famous for their celebrations, including San Joaquín de Flores in Heredia, San Francisco de Dos Ríos in San José, and the city of Cartago.

Hordes of secular *Josefinos* leave town for the week to enjoy a party atmosphere at the beach, traditionally the end of summer. This massive exit from San José actually creates a wonderful opportunity to stroll through the city without the normal hustle and bustle, and to enjoy its tranquil parks.

A typical Easter food is *chiverre*, a sweet jam made from a squashlike vegetable, which is used to make tarts, *empanadas*, or spread on home-baked breads. Sardines and seafood are also popular, since the religious tradition spurns the eating of red meat during this week.

Mother's Day

Although this is just a one-day celebration, usually at home with the family or at a restaurant, Mother's Day is an honored tradition in Costa Rica. Mothers throughout the country, as well as Mary, Mother of God, are given due respect on this day. It is also one of the best retailing holidays of the year, after Christmas. Love for Mom is the focus. There are many Ticos with an unknown or absent father, but just about everyone has a mother to celebrate with.

Independence Day

Independence Day is celebrated on September 15 with a relay race of student runners carrying the "Freedom Torch" from Guatemala to Costa Rica. The torch arrives at the colonial capital of Cartago at 6:00 p.m. the day before, when all Ticos join together in singing the national anthem. Children parade though the streets at night with *faroles,* homemade lanterns. The day itself is characterized by parades throughout the country with school bands and children in typical national costumes. Many people decorate their homes and businesses for the month of September with the Costa Rican flag, red, white, and blue streamers, and other patriotic ornaments. Costa Ricans are proud of their country and enjoy displaying their patriotism.

Day of Culture

October 12 was originally Columbus Day, celebrated to commemorate the Spanish conquest. Recently the name has been changed to The Day

of Culture, and indigenous protest marches as well as a Columbus celebration are now a feature. This holiday is most notable in Limón, where a *carnaval* lasts a full week, with colorful parades, concerts, dancing in the streets, typical Caribbean foods, and a festive atmosphere enjoyed by all. October in this area is relatively dry, which makes all-day and all-night outdoor celebrations possible. *Carnaval* draws many national and international visitors each year.

PILGRIMAGES AND FAIRS
La Virgen de Los Angeles
August 2 is the feast of *La Virgen de Los Angeles,* Costa Rica's patron saint, celebrated by a nationwide pilgrimage to the Basilica in Cartago. Inside the Basilica is the small statue of *La Negrita,* the black Virgin of Los Angeles, who is worshiped for her miraculous healing powers. The Basilica also houses an interesting collection of small, finely made silver and gold charms depicting different parts of the human anatomy, which are offered by the faithful in the hope of, or as thanks for, healing.

Pilgrims from all corners of the nation, as well as some from other parts of Central America, joyfully

make the pilgrimage to Cartago in honor of *La Negrita*. Many people from outlying areas start out at least a day before, walking through the night to arrive on August 2 to visit the small statue and offer prayers and thanks. Families, groups of friends, rich and poor alike, walk through the streets in this celebration. Most of the pilgrims are faithful believers, while many young people take advantage of the opportunity to spend a night out walking and partying with their friends. The streets are lined with food stalls, free water, and Red Cross stations to bandage blistered feet and attend to other problems. Many pilgrims choose to go the last hundred meters (about 300 feet) on their knees, as an act of devotion.

Fairs

A very popular tradition, with roots in colonial days, is the *turno*, or fair. Throughout the year, though more often in the dry summer months, small towns hold their annual *turno* to celebrate a patron saint or a religious holiday. The fair usually lasts at least a weekend, if not two. This is an important fund-raising event for the community church and school, and is made possible by the voluntary time and effort of the townspeople working together to make a party atmosphere. The proceeds are used for school or church maintenance and building projects, such as extra classrooms or the priest's house.

Small rustic booths are constructed of bamboo or other readily available materials to house the games and food stands. The games are varied but usually offer ball tosses, lucky-number wheel spins, climbing a slippery pole (*vara de fortuna*), and guessing the number of beans in a jar. Raffles are also popular. Bingo is an integral part of any *turno,* and is a proven way to gather young and old to try their luck. Buy a card, and you'll be given a handful of dried corn to mark the numbers.

Traditional foods draw a big crowd. A delicious array of homemade offerings includes rice and beans, corn on the cob, *picadillos* (a vegetable hash), grilled meat, and *prestiños* (a pancakelike treat covered with a sweet, sticky syrup).

La Mascarada is a parade of giant masked figures ranging from the diabolical and grotesque to the comical. These monstrous characters, *payasos,* run after the children, threatening to hit them with socks filled with sand or sawdust. Small towns usually have their own traditional *payasos*, which they bring out for the *turno*. The town of

Barva de Heredia is famed for the production of these gigantic papier-mâché creations.

The parade of *payasos* wouldn't be complete without the *cimarrona,* a local band. The music of the *cimarronas* is the best example of a continuing oral tradition. The enthusiastic participation of the townspeople is an important part of it.

The *carrera de cintas* is another traditional activity. This is a contest of horses and riders who ride past a line of hanging rings at high speed, and compete to hook a javelin into a ring. This event is lively, and often accompanied by high-spirited, cheering, and usually drinking supporters.

The *reinado*, or queen-crowning ceremony, is an important part of the traditional fair. Girls compete to collect the most money for the cause, and the winner is crowned queen of the festivities.

Veteran cowboys are experts at the public recitation of *bombas*, which are short, earthy, usually comic, and often risqué rhymes from the

Guanacaste cowboy culture. They are favorites at rowdy outdoor festivals. *Bombas* is also the name for the loud firecrackers that have been used throughout history to announce the start of local fairs. Even today these traditional noisemakers are used to announce the fairs, often as early as 5:00 a.m. It's not unusual for visitors, unaware of the custom, to think the noise is gunshots.

All these activities are occasions for a community to mix, party, and support its church and school. Throughout the country these *turnos* offer visitors a wonderful cultural perspective and a great opportunity to join in the fun.

QUINCE AÑOS
The *Quince Años* is a traditional celebration for girls when they turn fifteen, being their rite of passage from girl to woman. It usually consists of a mass, *misa,* followed by dancing, food, and festivities at home with family and friends, with the party girl traditionally wearing a pink dress. Today, many city girls opt for a more modern celebration, but out in the countryside, this tradition is still kept. Boys may also have a special party when they turn fifteen, but it is never the all-out celebration dedicated to the girls.

THE DECORATED OXCART
One of Costa Rica's national symbols, the colorful and intricately painted oxcart, *carreta de bueyes,*

represents the nation's agricultural roots. It played an important part in the country's economy, hauling loads of coffee to the ports. Oxcarts were a common sight until a few decades ago when trucks took over their role. Today in rural areas you can still see a few typical oxcarts in use.

The cultural and historical significance of the oxcart is celebrated each March on the second Sunday of the month, in Escazú. A colorful parade and a blessing of the animals and crops characterize the festival.

The artisan town of Sarchí is famous for making these typical oxcarts, from tiny souvenirs to large farm carts. Several of the workshops are open to the public, and you can watch the craftsmen working on the brightly colored, hand-painted designs.

chapter four

MAKING FRIENDS

Costa Ricans are famous for their warm hospitality, friendliness, and sociability. There are no strict social barriers to break through, and taking full advantage of these Tico characteristics makes it easy for a foreigner to find friends. While Costa Ricans may be too shy to initiate a conversation with someone new, the ice only needs to be broken. Go ahead and start talking to someone—it will usually be well received, and may be the start of an interesting and enjoyable relationship. Whether at work, study, or out and about, the opportunity to make friends awaits you.

The tropical climate encourages a relaxed, outdoor lifestyle. People tend to congregate in the parks, and meet in restaurants and cafés along the streets. If you are working or studying in Costa Rica, you can start socializing with your colleagues and classmates. It's easy to get on friendly terms. Costa Ricans enjoy going out with a group of friends and once you have been introduced, you will be invited to join the group. Certainly a display of outgoing friendliness will be reciprocated.

Though English is becoming increasingly common in tourist areas, in business, and around universities, and Ticos who have even a basic knowledge of English are always happy to practice it with you, most speak only Spanish. Feel free to try out your Spanish to communicate, however imperfect. Any mistakes on your part will be completely forgiven as people will appreciate your attempt to talk with them in their own language, and will enjoy the opportunity to communicate. Remember, if you want to meet the local people, go where they go, and use local stores and restaurants. If you spend all your time in tourist areas you will miss out on the opportunity of a rich cultural exchange with Costa Ricans.

THE NEIGHBORS

People tend to feel most at home in their own surroundings, so your local Costa Rican neighborhood is a great place to meet local Ticos in a comfortable, informal atmosphere. Use local stores on a regular basis, and everyone will soon get to know you. The local *pulpería* (general store)

is not only a source for all your basic food and household necessities; it is a great information center for what's going on in the area. People come for their daily shopping and always find time to chat. Make a daily appearance there. Your patronage will be appreciated, and you will soon be recognized and treated as a regular.

Moreover, as a foreigner you are interesting. People will be curious about where you are from, what your country is like, and what you think of Costa Rica. Take advantage of this opportunity to practice your Spanish and create a useful exchange of information. Make the effort to be friendly, and you will be rewarded with a satisfying group of friends.

If you are staying for a while, and have children, enrolling them in the local public school will help you to become immersed in the local community. Many social functions revolve around the school. You could also find out what ongoing school and community projects there are, and volunteer to help. Offering English tutoring is another good way to meet local people.

INVITATIONS HOME

In accordance with their friendly nature, Ticos readily invite their foreign friends to their home. If you are invited for dinner, it's usual to take a small gift, such as flowers, a bottle of alcohol, or some fresh bread or pastries. Don't arrive early, or exactly on time—any time up to thirty minutes after the appointed hour is acceptable. People at home tend to dress casually, and will expect you to do the same. Even at weddings and special celebrations the dress code is normally more casual than formal. Topics of conversation can safely revolve around the family, Costa Rica, or your home country. Conversations about religion or any kind of criticism of Ticos or their culture can be insulting to your hosts.

LEARN THE LANGUAGE

If you want to become immersed in Costa Rican culture, learning at least some Spanish is a must. Language schools abound in Costa Rica—in the cities around the Central Valley, and in tourist areas at the beaches and in the mountains. They usually offer an intensive basic course consisting of daily classes for a half day. Many offer weekend excursions, other activities, and opportunities to mix with Costa Ricans. A two-week basic course in grammar and conversation should give you enough confidence with the language to practice with the locals. Always keep in mind that practice makes perfect.

Some language schools offer English classes for Ticos as well as Spanish for foreigners. Many language students look for an interchange, *intercambio,* of language, where both parties have the chance to perfect the language they are studying in an informal setting. Take advantage of this opportunity, and you might make a good friend while you are doing it. Face-to-face, one-on-one communication can be a great way to learn with someone who has the time, patience, and desire to help you.

Homestays—living with a Costa Rican family—are another excellent option offered by many language schools. This is an affordable way to experience local customs and be involved in family gatherings and a Tico lifestyle. It provides a useful source of income for the host family, who enjoy learning about another culture from the guest, who in turn gains a direct insight into Costa Rican life.

FOREIGN STUDENTS

During the past decade there has been a huge increase in foreign students who have come to study in the Costa Rican national universities. These students normally have a very good grasp of the Spanish language, since the majority of their classes are taught in Spanish. Their situation in a foreign university has immersed them directly into the Tico culture. You can take advantage of their knowledge of Spanish and their Tico acquaintances to make both Costa Rican and English-speaking friends. The foreign students seem happy to communicate with someone in their native language, and can be a good source of information and a useful bridge for crossing over into the Tico culture.

High-school student exchanges have also become popular recently, though they tend to be for shorter periods of time. The students usually come for a few weeks to a month, and it's more like a vacation than a study program. Most of the students are placed with Tico families for full immersion into the culture. The host families are always delighted to open their homes to the students.

CLUBS AND GROUPS
Expatriate Clubs

Costa Rica has a vast number of expatriate clubs. Your embassy will have a list of these. It's generally considered a good idea to register with your embassy and take advantage of the useful information it provides, and this is a good way to learn from others about the country firsthand. From hiking groups to computer clubs, there seems to be something to satisfy everyone's desires. Some are charitable organizations; others simply offer social gatherings to share common interests. Even if you'd prefer to socialize with Costa Ricans, expats, with years of experience of living in the country, may be a good source of introductions to local people who share your interests. And if you don't find what you are looking for, why not start a new club?

Sports Clubs and Other Groups

Joining others in an activity you like is a good way to practice your Spanish and to enjoy yourself. There are a few public tennis courts available, numerous soccer fields, and some golf courses, open to the public. A game of chess or checkers can be enjoyed in the park or at a café. Soccer matches draw huge crowds to the stadiums, or you can watch the game live on a wide-screen TV at a sports bar. Soccer fans will have no problem meeting friends here. Most towns, whatever their size, have their own local soccer team that plays on Sundays. Female teams are becoming increasingly popular. In the past few years a new sports rage has been spreading through the Central Valley. *Futbol 5* is an indoor soccer game played with a smaller ball and on a smaller pitch. Join in with a few locals for a couple of hours of indoor soccer.

Basketball is also popular, with baskets located in many parks and schools. It is second in popularity only to soccer, and is the only other televised team event.

Numerous fitness classes, from *tai chi* to aerobics, are readily available and are a good way to meet friends and keep exercised. Gyms are widespread throughout the country. There is usually a small monthly fee.

The great outdoors offers wonderful hiking trails, swimming in the sea, rivers, or public pools, bicycle riding, horseback riding, and camping. The Ticos take full advantage of their idyllic climate for fresh-air sports and activities.

Another great option for meeting friends is to dance! You can learn Latin, Caribbean, Flamenco, or classical dance at any one of the growing number of dance schools. Many of the language schools also offer dance classes. The Ticos seem to have a natural talent for dancing. From early childhood they are taught traditional folk dances, and dancing is a common activity at any festive gathering. Learn to shake your body and shed your inhibitions while making new friends on the dance floor!

ENGLISH-LANGUAGE PUBLICATIONS

There are a number of English-language publications in Costa Rica. These are useful sources of information for news, activities, and classified ads for employment, real estate, vehicles, and lonely hearts. Below is a list of what's available.

Tico Times: Central America's leading English-language weekly newspaper, published on Fridays. An on-line version is available at www.ticotimes.net.

Costa Rica Quarterly: a newsletter on travel, living, and retirement in Costa Rica.

Tico Trader: a tourist magazine focusing on the Pacific coast.

Costa Rica Traveler and *Costa Rica Outdoors*: bimonthly tourist magazines.

Business Costa Rica: the monthly business magazine of the American Chamber of Commerce in Costa Rica.

A.M. Costa Rica: an on-line newspaper, at www.amcostarica.com.

La Nación: Costa Rica's best Spanish daily, with an on-line English version available at www.nacion.com/In_ee/english.

COSTA RICANS
AT HOME

Today most Costa Ricans live in towns and cities around the Central Valley. Slightly more than half of the country's four and a half million people live in cities, as opposed to only one-third in 1970.

COSTA RICAN HOMES

Most Ticos around the Central Valley and out in the *campo* live in houses. Whether the house is small or large it is home, and a source of pride to its owners. The traditional old colonial adobe houses

and the typical brightly painted all-wooden houses are slowly disappearing and being replaced by cement block or concrete and steel structures. Some of the beautiful old colonial homes have been restored and remain as a link to the past.

Costa Ricans are very meticulous about their homes. Houses are frequently freshly painted and the ornamental gardens tended with care. The floors inside, whether of wood or ceramic tiles, are highly polished. Pride is taken in maintaining the home's spick-and-span presentation.

Around the Central Valley, as land prices increase, apartments and condominiums are becoming more popular. They offer a more affordable and often a more secure option, though many lack any kind of yard or green area.

It is quite common for Costa Rican homes to have their outer walls touch their neighbor's. People take full advantage of the size of their lot, and often build to the boundary of the property, leaving no space between the houses.

Almost all wealthy and many middle-class Costa Ricans own a plot of land out in the countryside. They use their rural property for the weekends and vacations, a place to get away and relax. Whether they have a small beach cabin or a luxurious mountain home, the Ticos take full advantage of enjoying their time off in their home away from home. Many a family *quinta* (country house), or *finca* (farm) is planted with fruit trees, coffee, or vegetable crops. Harvest time is another good reason to head to the country.

Rental houses, apartments, and even rooms are readily available at a wide variety of prices. The most desired beach areas and the town of Escazú near San José compete for very high rents, while elsewhere rents are usually very affordable.

The Household

Generally speaking, the woman runs the house. Today nearly 60 percent of mothers are single heads of households, but even when the man lives at home, the woman is the strong and articulate manager of the families' life and budget. Women keep their homes sparkling, helped by their daughters. Living up to their *machismo* image, husbands and sons traditionally don't help with "women's work," but today, with many women working full-time, and influenced by the social changes of globalization, the men are beginning to lend a helping hand.

The Tico diet is built on a base of rice and beans. The classic breakfast of *gallo pinto* (rice and beans cooked together, and spiced according to the cook's desire) is still very popular. Fresh bread from the local store is also a basic, along with freshly brewed coffee. *Tortillas* with *natilla,* or sour cream, are a traditional breakfast out in the *campo.* The main meals of lunch and dinner typically consist of rice, beans, vegetables, meat, chicken, or fish, and salad. Soups are also very popular, and along the coast there is plenty of delicious fresh seafood available. *Tortillas* often form part of a meal, though fewer women have time to make them from scratch nowadays. Fresh tropical fruits are often enjoyed in fruit drinks, *frescos,* which accompany a meal.

The mid- to late-afternoon coffee break can almost be regarded as another meal. It's a great time to sit around and chat over a cup of the strong brew and a snack. The coffee is usually served with either fresh bread, a tortilla with cheese, *gallos,* which are tortillas filled with just about anything savory, sweet bread, or cake. An invitation from your neighbor to drop in for a *cafecito* will give you an excellent opportunity to practice your Spanish as well as to catch up on the local happenings.

Generally Costa Ricans don't sit down and share a meal as a family on a regular basis. With everyone on a different work or study schedule, they tend to eat when they get the opportunity. Pots of rice, beans, and whatever else are cooked daily and heated up as needed throughout the day.

Agua dulce, a hot drink made from an unprocessed sugar (*tapa dulce*) and water, is a traditional drink and also serves as a substitute for those who don't drink coffee. In this nation where coffee is king, coffee is often served, heavily sweetened, to small children and even in baby bottles. Over the past decade concerns have been raised about health issues caused by coffee, and this has led to some consciousness of caffeine consumption. Moderation appears to be the key, as the great majority of Ticos still thoroughly enjoy their traditional rich *cafecito.*

EVERYDAY SHOPPING

In the cities and larger towns most commercial businesses open at 9:00 a.m. and close at 5:00 or 6:00 p.m. Traditionally stores closed for a few hours at midday for lunch, but this custom is fading out. Many family-owned businesses in small towns still close from about 12 noon to 2:00 p.m., giving time for lunch and a *siesta.* Outside the city there are many smaller businesses that are open only half a day on Saturday. Sunday remains a day of rest, with most businesses closed, except for supermarkets and restaurants.

The local general store, *pulpería,* found throughout the country, opens by 6:00 a.m, giving people time to buy freshly baked bread and whatever else they need for breakfast before heading out to work or school. Many small stores and family-owned businesses outside the large towns tend to open by 7:00 or 8:00 a.m. The local *carniceria* for meat, the *panadería* for bread and bakery items, and the *verdulería* for fruits and vegetables do a thriving daily business. Many women choose to buy their bread, meat, and vegetables on a daily basis at their favorite local stores. Supermarkets are useful for basic food and household needs on a weekly or biweekly schedule, but can't replace the small local businesses for fresh daily supplies. In larger towns the Central Market offers a wide variety of booths selling fresh meat, cheese, fruit, and vegetables, and many other items. The open-air farmer's markets usually held on Saturday or Sunday are very popular.

Some businesses have a system of numbered tickets for customers to take when it gets busy, but people usually just crowd around and wait their turn to be served. The clerk appears to have a good sense of who's next, and tends to keep everyone happy.

In tourist areas business hours vary, with stores staying open until 8:00 or 9:00 p.m. Stores also open on Sundays in tourist areas during the high season.

Short banking hours have become a thing of the past. Many banks open by 9:00 a.m. and some stay open until 5:00 or 6:00 p.m. ATM machines offer service twenty-four hours a day and are becoming more widely available.

DAILY LIFE

Most Ticos start their day early. With school classes beginning at 7:00 a.m., people are up and moving by 5:30 or 6:00 a.m. Many workers use the bus for their daily commuting, so need plenty of time to get to their destination by 8:00 or 9:00 a.m. Though the bus service is widespread, inexpensive, and gets you where you want to go, it is slower than a car. The morning rush hour can cause staggering delays; so only by allowing extra time can you be assured of a prompt arrival.

Breakfast is typically a simple affair, with coffee and fresh bread. Children usually eat a heartier meal of *gallo pinto* with eggs or cereal. Coffee is the normal hot drink, though the children also enjoy hot chocolate or *agua dulce*.

The day's cooking begins early to prepare packed lunches. Rice, beans, meat, and vegetables are neatly packed into containers and usually heated up in a microwave at lunchtime, or eaten cold if one isn't available. Though restaurants do a thriving lunch business with the locals, just as many people bring their own homemade lunch. Daily dining at a restaurant, or even in a small *soda*, the most basic eating establishment, cuts deeply into a modest salary that has to stretch a long way. Those who live close to their work will lunch at home, though with the increasingly longer commutes to work, this practice is declining. At the end of the workday, by 5:00 or

6:00 p.m., those traveling by bus tend to head for home, usually expecting traffic jams. After dinner there's time to relax, watch TV, or unwind in the manner of your choice. Many university classes are held at night to enable young workers to further their education and be better able to compete in the job market. Classes usually last until 9:00 or 10:00 p.m., which makes for a full day.

Life in the Central Valley is becoming more competitive for children in school, for admission into university, and in the job market. Only in the outlying regions do you still find a tranquil country life. In the country the people still tend to live by the "early to bed, early to rise" philosophy. They work hard during the day and fully enjoy quiet evenings of relaxation.

EDUCATION

Education is a priority for Costa Ricans. In the city it has always been important; less so, traditionally, in the countryside. Even a few decades ago, many girls in rural areas attended only elementary school, finishing after the sixth grade. They were then expected to help out full-time at home. Attitudes have changed drastically in recent years, with a very high percentage of children, both girls and boys, from urban and rural areas alike, finishing high school and going on to university.

Costa Ricans realize the importance of a good education to enable them to compete in today's job market. Many parents who did not have the opportunity to go on to higher education want their children to be better educated.

The public school system is free and covers the whole country, with a number of one-room schoolhouses in isolated areas. All students in the system wear a school uniform. Many people take advantage of the free public schooling, though private schools have become increasingly popular in the last decades. Some people feel that the more they pay, the better the education their children will receive, which is definitely not the case. It has become fashionable to say that your children go to an expensive private school.

Starting School

Obligatory school begins with kindergarten at the age of five. Many children, particularly those with working parents, begin earlier, in public prekindergarten or private schools. After kindergarten, elementary school goes through sixth grade. There is a national exam at this stage that must be passed in order to enter high school.

There are usually two sessions of classes. The school day begins at 7:00 a.m., and the first session lasts until 12 noon; the second is from 12 noon to 5:00 p.m. In many schools the children alternate between morning and afternoon sessions. Lunch is free in the public schools and breakfast is also served in many rural low-income areas.

English has recently been included in the public school curriculum, beginning in the first grade. The great influence of foreign tourism and the boom of the computer age has made the learning of English a priority, though many students still graduate from high school without much proficiency. Most private schools teach English and possibly another foreign language.

High School

There are two kinds of high school—the preparatory and the technical. The preparatory goes from grades seven to eleven. The technical adds another year, ending with grade twelve. Both schools give a national exam during the last year, the *bachillerato,* which must be passed in order to graduate from high school and go on to university.

The preparatory schools usually have a schedule from 7:00 a.m. to mid-afternoon, with variations. Technical schools start at 7:00 a.m. and finish classes at 5:00 p.m. The study days are long and often include some hours of homework.

Some students manage to find time for extracurricular activities such as sports, music, and language or computer clubs. All public high school students must complete a required number of community service hours before graduating. These hours can be completed in a variety of ways, for example, volunteering in the national parks, at homes for the aged, or in campaigns to clean up rivers, beaches, and parks.

The Tico school year begins in February and finishes in mid-December. Some private schools follow a United States or European schedule, beginning in August or September and finishing at the end of May or early June.

Tertiary Education

There are four national universities, with fierce competition for admission. The Universidad de Costa Rica (UCR) is the biggest. It is located in San Pedro de Montes de Oca and offers a wide variety of careers in four-year and postgraduate studies. It also has campuses in San Ramón, Turrialba, and Puntarenas. The Universidad Nacional (UNA) in Heredia offers four-year and postgraduate studies with campuses also in Pérez Zeledón. The Instituto Tecnológico de Costa Rica, ITCR, in Cartago offers four-year and postgraduate programs and has campuses in San Carlos and San José. The Universidad Estatal a Distancia (UNED) offers four-year study at home courses and postgraduate courses, with centers in thirty places around the country. Numerous private colleges have sprung up over the last ten years to help fill the gap for the thousands of graduating high school students who want to continue with a university education and can't find a place in the public universities.

Government grants are given to needy elementary and high school students to cover the costs of a uniform and supplies. University scholarships are readily available to those students who earn them through merit and those who are in need of public assistance.

NAMES

Another tradition worth mentioning is the Ticos' use of two last names. Everyone uses their father's last name, followed by their mother's last name. When a woman marries, she usually keeps both of her parents' names. Sometimes a woman decides to use her husband's name by adding her husband's father's name on to her last name, with the addition of "de," for instance, Cristina Alvaro Ramirez, who weds Emilio Sanchez Mesén, would become Cristina Alvaro de Sanchez. This custom is disappearing as women choose to keep their own family names. The children from this marriage will receive the last names from the father of the father and mother. For example, Cristina and Emilio's daughter might be named Juana Sanchez Alvaro. Therefore, in any given family, the father, mother, and children will all have different last names.

When you ask a Costa Rican for his or her name, you will get the full name, which may be a long string of syllables. So, be prepared to listen well if you want to catch it all. Once you have learned the full name it is usually acceptable to converse on a friendlier, first-name basis.

Don and *Doña*

The familiarly courteous titles *Don* and *Doña* are commonly used instead of the more formal *Señor* and *Señora*. At the time of the Spanish conquest, these titles were used for people of noble lineage, but nowadays they are used as a polite way to address anyone who isn't a close friend. They are used by all classes. Unlike *Señor* and *Señora,* which are used with a last name, *Don* and *Doña* are used with a first name, such as *Don* Abel or *Doña* Juana.

chapter six

TIME OUT

Costa Ricans spend a great deal of their free time with their families and friends. During the dry summer months they love to be out of doors. City parks, national parks, and many private recreational areas are a big draw for people who want to relax and enjoy the fresh air, the trails, and the country's magnificent flora and fauna. Bicycling and ATV (all terrain vehicle) exploring are also popular leisure activities.

City people who have a second home in the country tend to go there for their time out. With two coasts of tropical beaches, many head to the seaside for diversion. The mountains are also popular, with many small cabins for rent, along with some luxurious hotels.

Because Costa Rica is relatively small, journeys by road usually take no more than a few hours, despite the road conditions, which are sometimes bad. The crowds of people who go out of the city for the weekend may leave at different times, but can cause massive traffic jams late on Sunday afternoons when they're all coming home again. Domestic flights can reach many destinations in less than an hour.

The week between Christmas and New Year is a very popular vacation time, as well as Holy Week and the first two weeks in July, when there is a school holiday. Whether vacation time is available or not, weekends and evenings readily serve for time out.

SHOPPING FOR PLEASURE

Shopping is a favorite pastime for Costa Ricans. San José offers the widest choices of large department stores, fashion boutiques, and just about anything you could need or dream of. The towns of Heredia, Alajuela, and Cartago also have good shopping centers. Many small towns have bazaars that offer a wide variety of items. The convenience of shopping nearby plus the idea of supporting a local business make these small concerns very popular and successful. Most stores in downtown areas are closed on Sundays. Some open a few Sundays before Christmas for shopping convenience.

A great attraction for Tico shoppers over the last ten years has been the opening of numerous malls. The biggest of these is Multiplaza-Escazú. People enjoy the architecture and interesting layout of the malls, and the great diversity of shopping experiences under one roof. A mall usually has at least one large department store, a grocery store, numerous clothes and shoe stores, specialty shops, restaurants, and a large food court with numerous fast-food options. An additional draw is the movie theaters, usually six per mall.

Most malls are located just outside the cities, which helps to ease traffic flow in the city, but be prepared to hunt for a place in the packed parking lots. Weekends are the busiest times, and all the stores in the malls open on Sundays. Many people go for the whole day, just to window-shop, sample the food, and enjoy the social atmosphere. Ticos have adapted well to the mall culture that globalization has brought. In most of the major shopping centers you will find a bookstore from the Librería Internacional chain. These carry a wide selection of books in English and Spanish.

Outdoor markets and craft fairs are popular with Ticos and tourists alike. Purchasing handcrafted items can be an interesting and affordable cultural experience, and buying directly from the artist is satisfying for both buyer and seller. Good-humored bargaining at outdoor markets is acceptable, but remember that the markup may be modest, so don't normally expect to pay less than 75 percent of the original price. Many fairs also have live music and food booths.

The increasing number of large chain stores that offer a huge variety of imported and specialty goods are popular with both residents and visitors. Gone are the days when choices were few and far between. The Ticos thoroughly enjoy increasing the national consumption.

EATING OUT

Costa Ricans enjoy going out to eat, whether for a quick drink and *boca* (literally, a little mouthful of food), a *cafecito,* or a full meal on a special occasion. Restaurants abound, from small *sodas* (very basic) to large, expensive establishments. Fast-food chains from the USA are widespread.

Bars traditionally serve a complimentary *boca* with an alcoholic drink. This is a tasty snack, such as a small *tortilla* with cheese, *chicharrón* (similar to thick bacon), chicken wings, fried cheese, or *ceviche* (raw fish marinated in lemon juice). A few beers and *bocas* can make a meal. The bars on the weekends draw crowds of Ticos looking for satisfying food, drink, and entertainment.

Small *sodas* usually open early in the day to provide breakfast for people on the move. Lunch is also available, usually offering a *casado*—a plate of rice, beans, cooked vegetable, and salad. *Olla de carne* is a popular meat and vegetable stew. *Sopa negra* is a tasty black bean soup, often served with an egg in it. Many *sodas* now serve more than the typical Costa Rican food, since hamburgers and fries are in demand.

The options for more expensive restaurants are numerous. Italian, Chinese, Middle Eastern, Mexican, French, and Indian cuisine, and seafood, can all be enjoyed in fine restaurants in San José and in many of the tourist areas. Most are open for lunch and dinner, and many close one day a week, usually on a Monday.

Good food need not be expensive—it can be found at a small *soda* off the beaten track as well as in an elegant restaurant. Typical food can be enjoyed for a very reasonable price. The central markets are a popular place for a bite to eat.

TIPPING

In restaurants, a 10 percent service charge, plus a 13 percent tax, is automatically added to the check. It is not customary to leave an additional tip, but if you feel the food and service were exceptional you can leave something extra on the table.

Taxi drivers are usually not tipped, unless you hire a taxi for the whole day, when it is customary to give the driver an extra 10 percent. Tips should also be given to bellboys at hotels, porters at the airport, hairdressers, and car attendants, who watch your car on the street.

FOOD AND DRINK

Costa Ricans enjoy all aspects of food, from the loving preparation of a meal to the satisfying consumption of it. Despite the increasing popularity of widespread fast-food chains, Ticos will admit that nothing beats a typical homemade meal. Costa Rican food specialties traditionally come from the different regions of the country.

The basis of the Costa Rican diet is rice and beans. Meat, chicken, or fish, and cabbage salad or other vegetables are added. At breakfast, lunch, and dinner it's not unusual to see rice and beans appear in some form. In general, the food is not spicy, but it can be jazzed up by adding *chilero*—hot chilies, onions, and carrots pickled in vinegar—or the popular Lizano bottled sauce.

Ticos eat a lot of chicken, roasted on a grill, fried or cut up in the popular a*rroz con pollo*, chicken with rice. Beef is also popular, eaten in slices or shredded to add to a *picadillo,* a mix of very finely diced vegetables and meat. Pork is eaten mostly as *chuletas,* pork chops, or shredded to add to the traditional Christmas *tamales.* *Chicharrone*, or fried pork rinds, are also favored.

On the coasts, of course, fish and seafood are especially popular, fresh from the sea. *Ceviche* is a common dish made of chopped raw fish, onions, garlic, and tomatoes in lemon juice. Lobster and shrimp can be enjoyed at what many foreigners consider a real bargain. A hearty *bouillabaisse* is rich in a variety of seafood and vegetables. Sea turtle eggs as well as turtle meat are available, despite the supposed protection of this endangered species. There are a growing number of mountain farms where you can go to enjoy the scenery, fish for trout, and have your catch cooked right there. This has become a popular day's outing for the locals.

Guanacaste makes the traditional large corn *tortillas* with yellow corn, rather than the white corn used to make smaller *tortillas* throughout the country. The region is also famous for its homemade bread baked in clay ovens out of doors. These dome-shaped ovens have also become popular for cooking pizza at tourist spots.

The Caribbean coast offers the biggest change in cuisine from the rest of the nation. Many of their Afro-Caribbean specialties are gently cooked in coconut milk for a rich and unique flavor. Ginger cake is another spicy specialty enjoyed along the Caribbean coast, as well as coconut cookies. Traditionally the residents of this coast have used a wide variety of medicinal herbs. These are available as herbal teas or fruit drinks in many of the restaurants. Seafood is also popular here, and of course this helps to support the local fishermen.

A traditional dessert throughout the country is *arroz con leche*, a sweet, cinnamon-flavored rice pudding. Custard (*flan*) is another favorite treat. Ice cream is often served with cubes of fruit-flavored gelatin, as a "fruit salad." Homemade ice cream on a stick is found in many of the *pulperías* in interesting flavors such as peanut and sour cream. The Tico *tres leches* is an intensely sweet cake made with three different kinds of milk. Most Ticos appear to have a sweet tooth and regularly enjoy *confites* (candies) of chocolate or hard candies. The old-fashioned sweet is a chunk of fresh sugarcane, which children still love.

In addition to coffee and *agua dulce*, hot chocolate is a traditional hot drink. Favorite cold drinks include tropical fruit juices blended with water or milk, as well as drinks made from powdered rice, corn, and peanuts. Oats and water blended together produce another tasty, refreshing, and healthy drink.

Alcohol

The state monopoly National Liquor Factory produces the country's official sugarcane liquor, called *guaro,* or Cacique, its brand name. This is the least expensive liquor available, and is unfortunately abused by many. It's still not uncommon to see men lying on the side of the road after a binge of *guaro*, usually after receiving their weekly pay. Rum is very popular, either mixed with Coca Cola or in tropical fruit cocktails. The brand names Centenario, Ron Rico, and Flor de Caña are all good brands of rum. You can even buy rum and coke in a can.

Ticos love beer, which is readily available throughout the country. Imperial, the nation's flagship local brew, has a label with a black eagle that you will see everywhere. Pilsen is more bitter; Bavaria is available in light and dark brews. The local brewery also bottles the famous Dutch Heineken, and there are other imported beers.

Wine is available, and is not often drunk, probably because it has not traditionally been produced in the country. A few very sweet wines made from blackberries or tropical fruits are made, and in the past few years a decent local wine made from grapes has appeared on the scene. Most of the good wines available here come from Chile, Italy, or California, and they are expensive.

Coffee liqueurs are distilled here, and make great mixers. The National Liquor Factory produces Café Rica, while Café Britt produces its own liqueur.

Home-brewed concoctions are found in rural areas. *Chicha* is fermented from corn, pineapple, or other fruits. *Vino del Roble* is a fermented sap of the oak tree and traditionally appears at country weddings or special celebrations. Stills making contraband *guaro* are quite commonly found in the countryside.

Ticos love toasting to celebrate the moment, and to wish good things for the future. A typical toast consists of the group raising their glasses together and saying *Salud!* (Health!).

Drunkenness is a growing problem. Numerous fatal traffic accidents have been caused by high levels of alcohol in the drivers. AA meeting places are common throughout the country, in even the tiniest towns, to help combat this. There are English-speaking groups available in some areas.

NIGHTLIFE

Bars, nightclubs, and discos keep the night alive in San José and in some tourist areas. In many bars, live music promises an enjoyable evening out. Talented local bands play a wide variety of music, including pop, reggae, jazz, folk, and Spanish and English rock. The music usually starts about 10:00 p.m. at the clubs.

Discotecas start earlier in the evening and continue into the early hours of the morning. Ticos love dancing, and it is a pleasure to watch their interpretations of *salsa, merengue*, and other typical Latin dances. Rhythmic movement almost seems intuitive in Costa Ricans. Dancing is a great way to meet the locals. The cover charge often includes a drink. Even out in the *campo*, weekend dances are popular at the *salon communal*, or community center, usually with music from a *disco movil* (mobile sound and light equipment). The dances are held both for entertainment and to raise funds for the local community.

Over the past ten years some wonderful international singers have been making the Costa Rican concert circuit. Pavarotti was here recently to a sold-out performance. While tickets to many of these grand performances are not cheap, they are probably much less expensive than their equivalent in Europe or the United States. Both the Teatro Nacional and the Teatro Melico Salazar are beautiful old buildings with great acoustics and are wonderful places to enjoy a concert.

Mariachis can be found nightly at La Nueva Esmeralda in San José. They can be hired per

song, or for a multi-song serenade by the hour. These bands play guitars, trumpets, violins, and accordions as accompaniment to their entertaining serenades. Originally Mexican, *mariachis* have become a popular tradition in Costa Rica, and Ticos love their mournful *ranchero* music. They are often hired for family celebrations, such as weddings, *quince años* parties, and even funerals.

Prostitution is legal in Costa Rica, and women and transvestites ply their trade on the streets and in some of the clubs. Prostitutes are legally required to hold an up-to-date health card, but don't rely on the validity of this. AIDS is a growing problem throughout Central America.

CULTURAL ACTIVITIES

The Instituto Costarricense de Turismo (ICT), the tourist office in downtown San José, has a wealth of information on local museums, galleries, places of interest, current events, and forthcoming attractions. Cultural activities are also announced in local newspapers.

Museums and Galleries

Museums display permanent and temporary exhibitions of art, science, religion, and history. Though the majority of the museums are in San José, many small historical towns have museums to preserve knowledge of the arts, crafts, history, and culture of the local area. Visiting the museums can give an enjoyable and educational glimpse into Costa Rican culture. The Museo Nacional, housed in the Bellavista Fortress in San José, offers displays of Costa Rica's history.  The Gold Museum, below the Plaza de la Cultural in San José, displays over two thousand pre-Columbian artifacts. The Jade Museum has pre-Columbian jade and stone artifacts, as well as gold. The Children's Museum, housed in the old men's penitentiary, has become a popular cultural center since it opened nearly ten years ago. It has a large auditorium for concerts and special events, an art library, gallery, and many interactive exhibits. The Museum of Costa Rican Art is located in La Sabana Park, which used to be the old airport. There is free entry to some of the museums on Sundays. Many are closed on Mondays.

Galleries are numerous in San José and Escazú, with some scattered through the tourist areas. They display a wide range of art, from traditional landscapes to abstract modern pieces. Artistic expression is encouraged in the Ticos from an early age, and inclusion of arts and crafts in their school program helps to balance the academic work. A growing number of professional artists have received both national and international acknowledgment.

Many cultural centers, such as the North American–Costa Rican Cultural Center and the Spanish Cultural Center, frequently host exhibitions, and often hold free parties—lively affairs with complimentary drinks and *bocas*, and another prime place to meet people. These centers also offer concerts, plays, classes, and other interesting cultural events, all listed in the daily newspaper.

Historic Buildings and Antiquities

Costa Rica has some unique historical structures that are well worth seeing. Unfortunately, many colonial buildings were destroyed by earthquakes or fell into disrepair. Ticos have a healthy respect for these windows into the past, and have recently started to put more energy into saving them.

Many of the remaining older buildings are churches, some dating back to colonial days. The Basilica de Nuestra Señora de Los Angeles, in the city of Cartago, is a work of art inside and out. It was rebuilt after the earthquake in 1926 on the spot where *La Negrita,* the church's namesake, had repeatedly appeared to a young country girl in 1635. As we have seen, Ticos faithful to *La Negrita* make a pilgrimage to honor her at the basilica each August 2.

The Church of San José de Orosí, in Cartago province, built in 1743, is the country's oldest colonial adobe church still in use. It houses a small museum of religious artifacts, wood carvings, and colonial furniture.

Many other churches throughout the country, both grandiose and diminutive in size, display beautiful architecture from the past, and are well worth a visit. The faithful have traditionally donated money to support the churches, and take great pride in their splendor. In all houses of worship you are expected to dress and behave respectfully.

There are several noteworthy buildings in San José, including the National Theater, funded by the coffee barons to promote high European culture. The theater is modeled after the Paris Opera House, and has a beautiful baroque interior. It is host to top national and international performers. The Melico Salazar Theater, built as the "people's theater," has elegant hardwood interior details. It presents many national and international artists. The Variedades Theater has been restored as a historical site, and continues to show contemporary cinema.

Walking through some of the areas around the city center, you will find some well-maintained and some restored old colonial homes, which help to create a picture of the past Costa Rican aristocracy. Some have been turned into hotels. The government is attempting to preserve and restore many of these historic colonial buildings as *patrimonio nacional*. Its efforts tend to involve a long, bureaucratic process that isn't always successful. These areas also give you an insight into the social structure of Costa Rican society, with elegant homes side-by-side with very humble constructions.

The Guayabo Archaeological Monument, located at the foot of the Turrialba volcano, east of San José, protects an important pre-Columbian archaeological site. This ancient city was built in stages, between a thousand and eleven hundred years BCE. Archaeologists believe it could have been continuously occupied until shortly before the arrival of the Spanish in the early 1500s. Guayabo is the only partially excavated major archaeological site open to tourists all year-round.

Ticos appear to be having a rebirth of their interest in their historical roots. With rapid changes in today's world they want to keep a firm basis in their cultural roots as Costa Ricans. They are proud of the differences that set them

apart from neighboring countries, and want to preserve and honor their unique heritage.

Theater, Opera, Dance, and Music
Costa Ricans are avid fans of a wide variety of theater. Playhouses offer anything from comedies about Tico daily life situations to Spanish and Shakespearean classical dramas. All performances are in Spanish, except for the English-language Little Theater Group, which produces a wide variety of comedies, dramas, and tragedies. Though most of the theaters are

in central San José, there are others in outlying areas. Live theater is a bargain in Costa Rica, a ticket costing only slightly more than admission to a movie.

Opera is performed by touring international opera groups, usually in the National Theater. The Ticos happily anticipate these performances, and reward their guests with a full house and appreciative audience.

Small ballet companies and excellent modern dance groups from the University of Costa Rica produce impressive shows. The National Dance Company presents colorful folkloric dances, musicals, and international artists. Costa Ricans appreciate the rhythm of dance and music from an early age.

There are many venues for enjoying live music. The National Symphony Orchestra is in residence from March to November. It is a splendid and widely traveled orchestra that in its home season hosts international guest conductors and artists. There are several music festivals throughout the year. The International Arts and Music Festival during March hosts both traditional and avant-garde talent. Affordable admissions allow a large cross-section of society to appreciate the festival. The South Caribbean Music Festival vibrates with reggae from March to May, also to support the children's music program.

Local bars and clubs put on live entertainment ranging from jazz, reggae, pop, and rock to folk. Listening to and becoming immersed in music is a Costa Rican passion.

Cinema

Most cinemas offer Hollywood movies in English with Spanish subtitles. Children's movies are dubbed in Spanish. The recent arrival of numerous theaters in the suburban malls, which continue to pop up, has created a boom in moviegoing. Many cinemas offer a two-for-one night on Wednesdays. El Semaforo, in San Pedro, shows only Latin American and Spanish movies. The Sala Garbo in San José specializes in cultural and international films. The University of Costa Rica also shows movies in the Law School auditorium throughout the academic year. The award-winning Costa Rican film *Caribe* continues to draw enthusiastic moviegoers.

SPORTS
Futbol

Costa Ricans are enthusiastic soccer fans. They love both to play it and to watch it on TV. Every little town has a soccer field, and children learn to play from an early age. What once was primarily a male sport is now attracting many female

players, and schools and communities have their
own girls' and women's soccer teams.

Costa Rica's national team is the Sele, which
proudly represents the country displaying the
flag's colors of red,
white, and blue.
The team has
played in two
World Cups and is
made up of the
country's best
players, many of
whom now play in
foreign countries.
When the national
team is not in
action the focus is
on the First
Division Teams from different regions of the
country. Twelve teams participate in this division,
with two of them dominating the lead. Alajuela's
La Liga and San José's Saprissa are archrivals,
with their faithful fans supporting them to the
end. When the two teams play the "Clasico," half
the country dresses in red and black to support
La Liga, while the other half dress in purple and
white to support Saprissa. Heredia, Cartago, San
Carlos, Liberia, Nicoya, and San Isidro de El
General also have teams with passionate local
supporters.

Sunday is the traditional day for football
matches, usually starting about 11:00 a.m., to avoid
disruption from afternoon rains. Games during the

week are played at night. The fans who fill the stadiums are cheerful and active, singing and leaping about throughout the game. Enjoying a soccer game with the locals is a memorable cultural experience.

Basketball

You will see hoops for basketball in many parks and school recreation areas, as well as strategically placed on the walls of houses and garages. Proper courts are hard to come by, but shooting baskets with the locals is an enjoyable pastime.

Outdoor Activities

Mountain biking has become very popular in Costa Rica, where the topography, forest cover, and weather combine to create great conditions for almost any skill level. On weekends, the hills above the Central Valley are filled with bikers. Several Ticos compete on the international circuit.

Camping is a low-cost way of enjoying the outdoors. Many Ticos flock to the beaches and mountains to enjoy camping vacations at all times of the year. Then there are numerous hiking trails in national parks, and private reserves that offer rewarding immersion in nature and majestic views. The Costa Rica Hiking Club organizes outings for the last Sunday of each month, and is a good source of information on hiking.

The early morning walking and jogging enthusiasts get their exercise along the sidewalks and streets of the cities and along country roads. They take advantage of the idyllic climate, and keep healthy in the process.

Golf courses have sprouted up around the country recently, offering residents and visitors a variety of public and private courses. It is advisable to make reservations, and to take a hat for sun protection, and drinking water.

While tennis has not traditionally been popular in Costa Rica, the success of the national ATP touring pro, Luis Alberto Marin, has inspired interest. Most tennis courts are in private clubs or hotels, but there is a public court in La Sabana Park.

Surfing the waves that bathe both coasts has traditionally drawn young local enthusiasts, and now tourism brings a steady stream of surfers in search of the perfect wave. The warm water is inviting, and wet suits are not required. Boards can be rented at most popular surf beaches and locals offer lessons.

If you are into adventure sports, the kayaking and whitewater rafting are wonderful. There is something for every skill level and preference, from fast-moving white water to tranquil floats through verdant jungles. Some of the locals like to ride huge truck inner tubes down the river.

With hundreds of resident bird species in this small nation, Costa Rica is popular with national and international bird-watchers. Spotting the brilliantly colored tropical birds is a truly rewarding experience. The Birding Club of Costa Rica organizes monthly outings with knowledgeable guides.

LOTTERY AND GAMBLING

The Costa Ricans are addicted to games of chance. The weekly national lottery draws enthusiastic players, the excitement of a possible win being well worth the risk of losing a few hundred *colones*. Just about everyone takes part in El Gordo, the biggest lottery of the year, played just before Christmas. The Junta de Protección Social de San José (JPS) runs the lottery and invests the earnings into much-needed social programs. So, even if they don't win, participants feel they are giving their money to a worthy cause. Lottery tickets can be bought on street corners throughout the country, the vendors ranging from small children to elderly men and women actively working to earn a living. The JPS is hoping to have an on-line lottery soon. Costa Ricans faithfully support the lottery for the ever-present possibility of winning the big one.

Casinos began to sprout up all over the Central Valley about ten years ago. Despite some political controversy, they have multiplied and are extremely popular. Most are located in large hotels and have expanded outside the city into the tourist areas. Perks vary, but many casinos offer players free transportation and drinks. Roulettes of different varieties are common, as well as *pai gao*, a Chinese poker game, which is growing in popularity. The local variation of *vingt-et-un*, called rummy, is a standard game in the casinos. International card tournaments are regularly hosted here. Some casinos have video poker as well as slot machines. Sports desks have become very popular, where gamblers can wager on US sports events.

ECOTOURISM

With the boom of ecotourism, Costa Rica has really found its niche. As a small tropical country, with two coasts and a string of mountains and

volcanoes in the center, it offers an amazing diversity of flora and fauna. National and international tourists are drawn to the national parks, private reserves, numerous nature recreation areas, and eco-lodges (see Chapter 7).

About a quarter of the country is now designated as national parks, private reserves, and conservation areas. Admission fees to national parks and many other tourist attractions are very reasonable. Group rates make the sites readily available to everyone.

Canopy tours, an increasingly popular attraction, give you the opportunity to ride, walk, and swing through the treetops, and to have unique views of the rain forest. There are hanging bridges through the rain forest canopy. Bungee jumping from the Rio Colorado Bridge is for the fearless, and the tour company also offers rappelling into the gorge.

chapter **seven**

TRAVELING

Traveling in Costa Rica is generally good, though road and weather conditions have to be taken into consideration. The road network throughout the country will take you just about anywhere, though there are areas where a four-wheel-drive vehicle is necessary. A direct bus will take you to your destination, generally in comfort, for a reasonable price and in good time. A long-distance bus journey can be an interesting cultural experience, giving you the opportunity to meet your fellow passengers, see the countryside, and stop along the way to experience the Tico culture firsthand. The national airlines fly to many destinations in a fraction of the time that it would take to drive there. The small, low-flying airplanes will also give you stunning views from the air. You can fly to any of the national destinations in less than an hour.

BY AIR

The great majority of the million people who arrived in Costa Rica in 2004 arrived by plane.

There are two international airports, the Juan Santamaría Airport just outside San José, and the Daniel Oduber Airport in Liberia. The Juan Santamaría Airport has been completely remodeled and enlarged in the last few years, to handle large numbers of tourists in the high season; but there are still congestion problems, caused by numerous flights scheduled for departure or arrival at more or less the same time.

Many airlines now fly into Costa Rica, with connections from all over the world. The Daniel Oduber Airport has become quite popular with those heading for the beaches of Guanacaste who don't want to go through San José. Significantly cheaper charter flights frequently fly into this airport with groups of tourists making for the sun.

National flights are handled by two domestic airlines, SANSA (using the Juan Santamaría Airport) and Nature Air (using the Tobias Bolaños Airport in Pavas). They use small planes carrying from four to fifteen passengers, and you can reach any of their destinations within an hour. The views from these lower-flying planes are impressive, and the air currents affecting the movement of the plane can turn the trip into quite an adventure. National airplane charter flights are also available, as well as helicopter charters.

BY CAR

The international Inter-American Highway extends from Peñas Blancas, near the Nicaraguan border, to the southern border with Panama at Paso Canoas. Some stretches of the modern *autopistas* have tolls. The (inexpensive) charges are posted on signs as you approach the *peaje* (toll booth). Go to the fast lane if you have the exact money, another if you need change.

Costa Rica is renowned for its hazardous and challenging road conditions. With the torrential rains, potholes, mudslides, curving mountain roads, and lack of lights and markings, roads should be used with care and moderate speed. Gravel roads abound, especially in outlying areas. Four-wheel-drive vehicles are popular for road trips outside the city, especially during the rainy season. There are numerous narrow, one-lane bridges—always check for oncoming traffic before crossing one.

Costa Ricans can be dangerous drivers, especially in the city, where there are more cars than the

streets can handle. Traffic jams in San José are a regular occurrence. Many Ticos don't pay much attention to the rules of the road, often behaving unpredictably and aggressively, and using their horns freely. Ideally, have a good map and a planned route when traveling by car.

Legal Requirements

Tourists wishing to drive in Costa Rica need a valid driver's license from their home country and a passport. This driving allowance is usually good for three months. The vehicle registration document must be available in the car along with an up-to-date *marchamo,* which includes the taxes for road use and the obligatory insurance, displayed on the right side of the windshield. The annual vehicle inspection by Riteve must also be up to date. Seat belts are required for all passengers. The legal age for getting a driver's license in Costa Rica is eighteen.

Traffic police use radar, and speeding fines can be expensive. If you are pulled over and fined for any traffic infraction, insist on being given the ticket, and pay later. It is illegal to pay on the spot. Bribes are also illegal, but still commonplace. If an accident occurs, don't move your car or let the other driver bribe you. Wait until a traffic officer arrives at the scene.

Particularly during holidays, traffic police are out in force, pulling drivers over to test them for alcohol. The legal limit of alcohol concentration in the blood is 0.05 percent. Less than that is considered sober; from 0.05%–0.1 percent is considered pre-intoxication; 0.1 percent or above is considered as intoxicated. A large number of fatal traffic accidents have been traced to alcohol abuse.

Motorists must not use a cell phone while driving. Though the practice of using one is quite commonplace, it is illegal.

RULES OF THE ROAD

- Drive on the right. Always give way to traffic entering from the right.

- The rotundas, or traffic circles, can be confusing. Give way to incoming traffic.

- Pay special attention to the placement of traffic lights; they may be hanging overhead or at the side of the road.

- Pedestrians don't have the right of way, and must be alert and decisive to cross the street.

- Flashing headlights are a signal from oncoming cars of something that needs your attention, such as police ahead, or an accident, so it is wise to slow down. Flashing lights or hooting from behind usually means "Move over!"—the car behind wants to pass.

- Costa Ricans often just decide for themselves to follow, or not to follow, the rules of the road. If they see no one coming when they have stopped at a red light, they often just drive on. This is only one small example of the diversity of divergence of rules and reality. Always drive with care.

- Expect the unexpected. You never know when you will find a tree fallen across the road, a funeral procession on its way to the cemetery, a mud slide, or pedestrians at the side of the road. Meet the challenges with intelligence and patience.

Parking

In San José there is very little free public parking. Also, car thefts are frequent and on the rise, so you should park in a private parking lot, where an attendant provides security, and don't leave any valuables in the car. If you park illegally in the city, you will probably return to find the car has been towed away. Getting it back can be time-consuming and expensive.

In other cities and towns, parking on the street in legally designated areas is usually safe for a short period. There is normally an attendant who will sell you a ticket for a certain amount of time and assure you that he'll watch your car. Small tips are paid to these attendants. Again, don't leave valuables in the car. Outside the cities you will notice that people tend to park just about anywhere. People commonly pull up on the sidewalk, double park, and block driveways. As long as it's not in anyone's way and you feel it's safe, all should be well.

Mall parking lots have become a target for car thieves, who are, of course, clever at their business. Despite the use of car alarms, steering-wheel locks, and other protective systems, the thieves unfortunately often succeed in breaking in. If your car is stolen, it may well not be recovered. Vehicles are expensive in Costa Rica, and the black market in stolen cars is booming.

BY TRAIN

Not long ago there was a train service to both coasts, but today the only remaining service is the Tico Train Tour to Caldera on Saturdays and Sundays. The train goes through Santa Ana, Atenas, and Orotina, leaving at 7:00 a.m. and returning at 4:30 p.m., giving you about five hours at the beach at Caldera.

There is also a commuter train service between San José, Heredia, and San Antonio de Belen. Although quite crowded at peak hours, the train provides a quick, inexpensive, and comfortable alternative to fighting the traffic jams into and out of the city.

INTERCITY BUSES

Throughout Costa Rica there is a vast bus network offering good and inexpensive travel. Most of the private companies have comfortable, well-maintained vehicles. On weekends and during holiday periods it's best to buy your ticket a day or two ahead to reserve a seat. The majority of intercity buses don't take standing passengers, though occasionally you'll see a few people standing for a short distance. Bus travel can be an enjoyable experience.

Indirect buses stop frequently, making the trip much longer, but direct buses are pretty time-efficient. On long trips the bus usually stops for a ten- to fifteen-minute refreshment break. Be sure to be promptly back on board.

URBAN TRANSPORTATION
Buses
The city bus system in Costa Rica is an important part of its lifeline. Many people use buses daily.

Even those with cars often prefer to catch a bus into the city to avoid driving in the jams and searching for parking. Buses range from the old school bus style to the most modern Mercedes Benz coaches, and are generally comfortable and in good condition. Fares are reasonable. Exact change is not necessary, but you should pay with coins or a bill of 2,000 *colones* or less.

These buses take as many people as can crowd in. In peak traffic time in the morning and at the end of the day, they can be very full, with long lines waiting. Priority, both legal and generally out of politeness, for seats is given to the elderly, pregnant women, and the disabled. To let the driver know you want to get off, pull the cord by the window and a buzzer will ring. Sometimes there is a button every few feet along the central aisle, which is used instead of the cord.

The different routes have their own schedules, but the buses generally start by 5:00 a.m., and continue to run until about midnight. Some run through the night. You don't usually have to wait for more than ten to fifteen minutes for a bus in town; some are very frequent. They run all day every day except Holy Thursday and Good Friday.

Onboard there are often vendors, selling pencils, pens, or other small items to help support a variety of charity organizations, such as homes for drug addicts. They give a short talk about their charity, and then offer their wares. Most items cost about 100 *colones*.

Taxis

Taxis are plentiful in the city and outlying areas. Fares are very reasonable within the metropolitan area, making it an affordable and convenient option for traveling around the city. Taxis are red, with a yellow triangle on the door. There are certain areas in town where the cabs congregate, awaiting a fare, but you can just stop one on the street. It should have a working meter, *maria,* which should be switched on.

When traveling outside the city many taxis don't use their meter, so be sure to agree upon the price to your destination to avoid any problems. This can be expensive. Tipping is not expected, although if you've hired a cab for the day, a tip of 10 percent shows your appreciation for the service.

Illegal taxis, called *piratas,* also ply for hire on the streets. Most of these look like ordinary private cars, and don't have meters. Sometimes they can be cheaper than legal ones, but you must agree on a price before you get in. If you are not happy with the price, hail another cab. Unscrupulous taxi drivers will overcharge when possible.

WHERE TO STAY

Costa Rica's booming tourist industry has brought great economic benefit to the country. Ticos now want to focus on offering better-quality services and improving the infrastructure. There is growing competition in tourism from other Central American countries, and this has caused Costa Rica to make quality a priority.

A great variety of accommodation is available throughout the country, from the small *cabinas* at the beach or in the mountains to the five-star hotels in all popular areas. During the high season or the holidays it's best to make reservations. Prices vary according to location and what is offered, but there is something to suit everyone's taste and pocketbook. Many hotels offer great discounts during the low season. The high season is from late November to April, and there is another short high season during July and August. Many Costa Ricans take advantage of the reduced rates during the low season to enjoy tranquil vacations without the crowds.

Hotels

Hotels throughout the country conform to international standards and have a five-star rating system. The buildings come in all sizes and shapes: some are restored traditional colonial homes, others have the most modern architectural designs. Many of the larger hotels have conference rooms that can be rented for business or social gatherings. Many of the smaller ones, especially outside the metropolitan area, are family-run and offer warm hospitality and a homely atmosphere. From luxury to budget accommodation, the hotels offer something to please everyone.

Apartotels

Around San José and at various tourist destinations, there are apartotels that can be rented daily, weekly, or long-term. These are a good option for anyone wanting to do their own cooking and having a place to call home. The apartotels are usually furnished with just about everything you'd need in a comfortable household.

Hostels

Hostels are a good option for budget travelers and those who want to mingle with people from around the world. Costa Rica offers more than two dozen hostels recognized by Hostelling

International (www.hostels.com). They usually have dormitory-style room**s** with shared bathrooms and the use of a kitchen where you cook for yourself. Hostels are popular with the young backpacking travelers.

Homestays

Homestays, or living with a Costa Rican family, have become a popular option for visitors who want to become immersed in the culture and practice their Spanish. It's a great way to become involved in traditional family gatherings and real Tico lifestyles.

Eco-Lodges

Eco-lodges throughout the country focus on environmental friendliness. Many of them use sustainable energy sources, such as solar or hydro-generated power. They are also conscious about recycling and waste disposal. Choosing to stay in one of these lodges helps to support the protection of clean water, fresh air, and the verdant forests. The Costa Rican Institute of Tourism has a five-leaf rating system for environmental friendliness.

HEALTH AND INSURANCE

Costa Rica has a public health care system that is among the best in Latin America. The Social Security System (*Caja*), the country's socialized medical system, has public hospitals and clinics nationwide. Paying the monthly insurance fees allows one to use the facilities. *Caja* insurance is available for tourists as well as residents. Emergency care is always available to those in need.

Private hospitals and consultants provide efficient personalized service that may be lacking in the socialized medicine system. Many doctors at the private hospitals and clinics speak English. Most international insurance is accepted at the private facilities. There are well-stocked pharmacies throughout the country, and pharmacists are helpful and ready to give advice. Many drugs can be sold over the counter without a prescription. Generic drugs are usually available more cheaply than brand-name drugs. Some pharmacies are open twenty-four hours a day.

Dengue, a virus transmitted by the mosquito, is a slight risk for travelers. Precautions include avoiding stagnant water, wearing long-sleeved clothing, and using mosquito nets when possible.

Water is potable in most of the country, but in remote areas and port cities it is recommended that you drink only bottled water, which is widely available, and don't add ice.

The intense tropical sun can cause sunburn, which can be prevented by wearing a hat and using a sunscreen.

Recently an anti-tobacco law was signed by the president, which prohibits smoking in bus and train terminals, public transportation, shopping centers, bars, and restaurants. It remains to be seen how thoroughly this new law will be enforced.

SAFETY AND CRIME

Costa Rica remains the safest country in Central America despite the influence of the thriving narco-trafficking industry in the area. Recently the presidents of Central America met to discuss the decriminalization of drugs as an alternative way to fight the losing war on drugs in the region.

In the cities take the same sensible precautions with your belongings that you would take anywhere else in the world. Pickpockets are common in crowds, so don't carry large amounts of cash or valuables with you, and be vigilant. Costa Ricans are targets too, though foreigners tend to stand out more, thereby becoming frequent victims. An insurance policy against theft may be a good travel investment.

Violent crime is not usually a problem for the visitor. There are some areas of San José that are best not traversed on foot at night. Use a taxi to avoid any problems.

chapter eight

BUSINESS BRIEFING

As we have seen, over the last couple of decades the Costa Rican economy has moved on from its traditional agricultural base. Although bananas, pineapples, and coffee continue to produce a significant income, agriculture has been overtaken by tourism and high-tech industries, which vie for the number-one spot. Tourism, with its focus on ecotourism, has given a substantial boost to the

economy. High-tech products, such as Intel computer chips, dental implants, and services such as call centers, are a major source of revenue. The country has a dynamic, diversified, and educated workforce with a proven track record, which has attracted a large number of foreign investors.

As foreign investment in the business sector continues to grow, both the Costa Rican government, via the Instituto Nacional de Aprendizaje, and the United States Embassy offer further education classes to help prepare today's youth and young adults for the many jobs requiring workers who are English- and technology-savvy.

Foreigners coming to Costa Rica on business are struck by the laid-back, *mañana* attitude of Costa Ricans, as well as by the vital importance of good personal relations for a successful outcome. Business dealings should be given time and patience, sometimes much more than you would expect. The time spent waiting for bureaucratic paper pushing to take its course can be beneficially invested in building good personal relations with your Costa Rican business partners.

Your contacts, and "who knows whom," can become a major part of your business success. Costa Ricans are warm and friendly, and want to socialize before getting down to business. They need to know you personally, not just as a bland representative of a faceless corporation. Personal relationships give importance to the business at hand, and personal contact must be maintained to keep the business moving.

COMPANY ORGANIZATION AND BEHAVIOR

Costa Rica has five different types of business corporations. The two most popular are the *Sociedad Anónima* (SA) and the *Sociedad de Responsibilidad Limitada* (SRL). Both of these types of business are stock held and have limited responsibility. The SA must have a board of directors. The SRL is allowed to have a sole manager.

The Costa Rican business week is based on a forty-hour week, as compared to the legal forty-eight-hour week for farmworkers. Most offices are open from 8:00 a.m. to 5:00 p.m. with an hour's lunch break. The traditional *siesta* no longer exists as Costa Rica has become competitive in the global business economy. Note that all government offices and many private ones shut down for the entire Holy Week (*Semana Santa*), and often between Christmas and the New Year.

Costa Rican company structure is definitely a "top-down" hierarchy. There are many old-established companies and family firms in which the president is the absolute controller and the one who makes all the decisions.

The Patriarch

Antonio started a *ferretería*, or hardware store, in his garage thirty-five years ago. Since then, as the local community has grown, it has flourished, and he now owns a substantial business, with his sons, daughter, and wife all working for him in the store. Antonio continues to hold the reins of power, but his sons are really the ones who run the show.

With increasing global influence on local business, however, the governing power in many companies is now being divided among the board of directors, rather than remaining in the hands of the traditional patriarchal boss.

Bureaucracy

Costa Rican bureaucracy can be hugely time-consuming. Any kind of documentation, decisions, or instructions must be written down and stamped *recibido* (received) before it becomes valid. Both legal and business documentation can take twice as long to process than you may reasonably expect. Patience and persistence pay dividends in doing business here.

English is widely used in business circles. During the last fifty years, the United States has been Costa Rica's most important business and agricultural partner. Though Costa Rican commerce is rooted in Spanish business structures, the US now has the greatest influence over local business and Costa Ricans typically follow US practices.

CAFTA, the Central America Free Trade Agreement, we have seen, was successfully negotiated in 2004 and ratified by the Costa Rican national assembly. Despite fierce opposition by small businesses, environmentalists, and farmers, it promises to elevate Costa Rica from the status of a developing to a developed nation.

The Human Response

In business the human dimension takes priority. If an employee has significant personal problems, the boss must immediately attend to this and do what is possible to help.

Personal loyalty and friendship are the bedrock of business relationships, with ability a secondary requirement. Good personal relations create connections for recruitment, and prospects for promotion are based as much on your personal relationship with the company as on your aptitude or qualifications for the job.

BUSINESS STYLE

Appearances are very important in Costa Rica. Despite the country's tropical climate, full business dress is worn, with formal business suits and ties for men and sober dresses or suits, with either skirts or pants, for women. Ticos are stylish and very meticulous about personal grooming and presentation, with elegant hairstyles, jewelry, and all the business paraphernalia of briefcases and laptops. The center of business is located in San José, where the climate is more temperate.

After formal introductions and first meetings, people usually relax and the atmosphere can become quite informal. Jackets can be removed in the office. Personal chitchat is a very important part of the lead-in to business dealings, and networking is definitely part of the job. Even a short conversation over coffee can count for much more than an extended exchange of e-mails. Phone calls can take the place of a face-to-face meeting in the case of long-distance communication. Personal contact helps to create a relationship built on trust—a good basis for any business.

THE BUSINESS RELATIONSHIP

Doing business in Costa Rica centers, therefore, on good personal relations and mutual trust, and accepting invitations is an important part of the networking process. Talking about your family and children with your counterparts will show your human side, and will demonstrate that you have roots in your own society. This will contribute to your business partner's estimation of you, and give you greater credibility.

A successful business relationship moves beyond the business context. If you can help your partner or his family in some way—such as arranging an introduction for his son or daughter to a person in your home country—this will help to foster relations in the longer term. Contacts are all-important—knowing and suggesting someone who can help out is part of the give-and-take.

Follow-up in a business relationship is also vitally important. Of course the personal touch is best, but phone calls are also rewarding. Patience in cultivating a good business relationship will be well worth the investment. Ticos need time to build a trusted relationship with their business partners. The hard-sell approach is not well accepted or trusted in Costa Rica.

FLEXIBILITY

Flexibility is an important concept for both the Costa Rican and the foreign business partners. Foreigners in business in Costa Rica must accept the fact that things may take longer, often much longer, than anticipated. "Tico time" typically delays any scheduled time from half an hour to an hour, and is a given in this society, as in most Latin American cultures. Highly punctual foreigners in Costa Rica usually specify "*hora gringa*" (Gringo time), or "*hora alemana*" (German time), when they want their visitors to show up on the dot. The time-consuming bureaucracy and paperwork can contribute to the well-known *mañana* syndrome. Even if it appears that nothing is being done, things may actually be in process, so be flexible with your time expectations.

Your Costa Rican counterpart will also be flexible, with all the multitasking and juggling of important issues. Personal contact once again can provide the impetus to getting something done, so keep reminding him or her of your requirements, and of your personal relationship. Continual checking up on progress is essential.

MAKING APPOINTMENTS

Remember not to schedule appointments around the Christmas and Easter holidays. Make your appointments well ahead of time, and confirm them a day or so before. Costa Ricans use the system of writing dates with the day first, followed by the month, then the year. For instance, January 25, 2005, would be written 25-1-05.

Although Costa Rican business is influenced by US business philosophy, don't be surprised if you are expected to accept "Tico time," and are kept waiting for your appointment. It's important to arrive on time even if you have to wait. Bring papers or a book, or read a magazine while you wait.

When you arrive for your appointment, announce yourself to the receptionist by giving her your personal business card. Business cards are an important aspect of earning respect and trust in your business. They should be printed in both English and Spanish.

COMMUNICATION STYLE

The personal touch in communication is a necessary part of a business relationship. In e-mails, it is important to start with a polite preamble asking about the family, sending congratulations on their successes, and so on. Getting straight to the point would be considered cold and rude. Continued warmth and friendliness are essential to maintaining trust. On the phone it is also important to remember the chitchat before getting down to business.

Not only business cards, but also other printed material should be in both Spanish and English to facilitate a smooth process.

MEETINGS

In Costa Rica meetings are always accompanied by refreshments, at the very least a *cafecito*, and most of the time and attention are given to personal matters. Once the business agenda comes to the table, don't be surprised by overlapping

> **TABLE TALK**
>
> Auriana, the North American editor of Central America's leading English-language newspaper, was invited to a 1:00 p.m lunch meeting to discuss business with a group of Costa Rican counterparts. She was delayed, and rushed to the restaurant, arriving only five minutes late, but feeling stressed and anxious.
>
> As it turned out, she was only the second guest to arrive, and the remaining twelve people turned up over the next half hour. They sat down, enjoyed lunch with lots of friendly, personal chitchat, and only when the last coffee cup was removed did the business agenda come into focus. The presentation lasted just fifteen minutes of the hour-and-a-half business luncheon—but the business agenda had been satisfied.

conversations, which are quite common and not considered rude. The chairperson will try to present his or her point of view in the most persuasive of ways. Questions, answers, and comments are all welcome, but not contradictions. Meetings are seen as a way to promote both the personal and the business agenda.

PRESENTATIONS

Costa Ricans rely heavily on power point presentations. An eye-catching and logical display

of your ides is important for
success. Visual aids such as
videos or overhead projectors
help to relay the main message
of a presentation, making it
interesting and easy to grasp. It is difficult to
hold a group's attention for more than half an
hour, so the presentation should be short and to
the point, leaving plenty of time for socializing,
commenting, and developing the message
following the presentation.

Remember to have all printed material of the
presentation and proposals in both Spanish
and English.

NEGOTIATIONS AND CONTRACTS

Negotiations are generally carried out in a polite
business style, reflecting that of Europe and North
America. Eye contact is important to gain trust.
An upfront presentation in negotiations is well
accepted, but a hard-sell approach is not. The
policy of taking time to develop the business
relationship should be continued during
negotiations and throughout the follow-up and
period of the contract. It is not unusual for a
foreign company to employ a Costa Rican to lead
business negotiations on its behalf.

PLANNING AND CONTROL

Contracts are overseen by the company lawyer.
Abiding by the contract is an integral part of the
business relationship, and it is important to ensure
that the process moves along as planned. However,
you will find that schedules and projections are
basically regarded as rough guidelines and that
your partners must be continually encouraged to
observe them. Planning and control have their
part in fulfilling a contract, but you should realize
that the time frame as well as other controlling
factors may have to change along the way. Don't
expect deadlines to produce delivery. With many
things in motion, a fixed deadline is hard to
achieve. Helping the process along by personal
calls or visits is the intelligent way to proceed.

Teamwork plays an important part in business.
Costa Ricans are generally seen as cooperative,
having been trained from schooldays onward to
discuss and divide up a project, and to work
together as a team.

BUSINESS ENTERTAINING

Socializing and entertaining are a vital part of a
business partnership in Costa Rica. Be prepared to
invest some out-of-office time on building good
business relations. Be on time for a business
luncheon, as the time allotted for the lunch break
may be limited.

Most business entertaining takes place in
the evening, with an invitation to dinner at a
restaurant. Whoever extends the invitation

pays. Spouses are usually welcome at business dinners, and building the personal relationship will take up most of the time. Only after coffee is served is it proper to begin the business conversation.

If your Costa Rican business partner invites you to his home for dinner, this is, of course, an honor, as it would be anywhere, and you should certainly accept. Take a gift of alcohol, chocolates, or flowers. Calla lilies, however, are not a good choice, being usually associated with funerals.

It is a good idea to repay your host and hostess at some point by extending a dinner invitation to them. This continuance of common courtesy is just another step in building a firm basis for your business.

GIFT GIVING

At the conclusion of successful negotiations, or if you are invited to your business partner's home, it is usual to give a modest gift. This serves as a sign of interest in maintaining good personal and business relations, and as a thank you. It is important that this token is not too valuable or it might be taken as a bribe. A suitable gift might be a bottle of alcohol, or something from your home country, such as an attractively illustrated book, a CD, or a craft item. If you yourself receive a gift, open it immediately, and appreciatively.

Bribery and corruption in business has been in the news in Costa Rica. Two ex-presidents were recently jailed for "gifts" received during successful business negotiations. Though corruption is still rampant, the government is striving to control it through stricter laws, vigilance, and bringing the perpetrators to justice.

WOMEN IN BUSINESS

According to a study by Geert Hofstede, a Dutch researcher who has analyzed how values in the workplace are influenced by culture, Costa Rican women in business are met with greater acceptance than in any other Latin American country. Despite this positive outlook, the reality of a *macho* society still influences the role of women. Traditionally men control the majority of senior business positions. Women's high qualifications and hard work are slowly being rewarded, however, and are leading to better positions in today's more modern society.

Costa Rica's CAFTA negotiations with the USA in 2004 were led by a woman. The team of negotiators worked to influence the government to get the best possible trade agreement for the country. The negotiations were successful, and it was ratified by the Legislative Assembly.

Costa Rica currently has a woman president and there is an increasing number of women professionals in the medical and business fields. These women expect and receive complete equality with men in their professions.

CONCLUSION

Business in Costa Rica is based on good personal relationships. It takes time to make that vital personal connection with all the necessary contacts. Patience and flexibility are needed to build the trust that is the foundation of all successful partnerships.

Once your Costa Rican partners have accepted you on a personal level, it is easier for them to accept your business proposals. Constant follow-up is necessary to keep things moving, and for fulfillment of contracts. For those who take the time to create the requisite personal relationships, the country is ripe for business success. Costa Ricans are wide open to new approaches in today's global market, and Costa Rica's home market is only just being discovered.

chapter nine

COMMUNICATING

LANGUAGE

Spanish is the official language of Costa Rica. It is also spoken throughout Latin America, as well as in certain states in the USA, such as Florida, California, Texas, Arizona, and New Mexico. Spanish is the official language of the Caribbean island of Puerto Rico, and is widely spoken in Morocco and the Philippines. Worldwide, Spanish and English compete for second place, after Chinese, as the most spoken language.

A Creole dialect is spoken in the Afro-Caribbean culture along the Caribbean coast. Though quite similar to English, it has a character of its own. Indigenous languages are used within the indigenous population. The indigenous tribes are trying to incorporate their native languages into the school curriculum for their own children, in an effort to hold on to and honor their culture, which is difficult in today's melting pot.

English is increasingly widely spoken in Costa Rica. With the boom in tourism and the technological computer culture, English is becoming increasingly important for job hunters. A bilingual speaker of Spanish and English has a better chance of landing a good job with a reasonable salary than someone who speaks only Spanish. For this reason, English has recently become part of the public school curriculum.

SPEAKING SPANISH

You are highly recommended to acquire at least a basic knowledge of Spanish if you plan to spend time in the country. Using Spanish will show your interest in the culture, and will be appreciated. Costa Rican Spanish is an "Americanized" derivative of Castilian. It is similar to the Spanish spoken in southern and western Spain, which uses the "s" sound, rather than the English "th" sound for the letter combinations *ce, ze,* and *za*. There is a slight difference in accent and vocabulary in various regions of the country.

Costa Ricans are always willing to help you practice your Spanish. It doesn't matter if you make mistakes. The Ticos appreciate your attempt to communicate with them in their own language. They love to talk and will do their very best to communicate with you, despite your stumbling Spanish. Remember that practice makes perfect.

A Spanish phrase book and a dictionary will help you get by. For a better grounding in the language, a beginner's Spanish course will be very fruitful, and will give you confidence.

Spanish Pronunciation

Spanish is easy to pronounce once you have learned the sounds of the letters. The alphabet is made up of twenty-eight letters: *a, b, c, ch, d, e, f, g, h, i, j, k, l, ll, m, n, ñ, o, p, q, r, s, t, u, v, x, y, z.* The consonants *b* and *v* are pronounced almost the same, as are *y* and *ll.* The letter *h* is silent.

Stress is also important, and there are rules for this which you will learn. Tapes or CDs of Spanish language lessons, or even Spanish songs, will help you to get a feel for the sound and pronunciation of the language.

FACE-TO-FACE

The easiest way to communicate in Costa Rica is face-to-face. Ticos gesticulate and talk with their whole bodies, so if you can see them their meaning is much easier to grasp than if you are having the conversation over the phone. They often stand quite close to one another, and frequently touch the other person for emphasis during a conversation. For example, if asking for agreement, they might tap or grasp an arm or shoulder and say, "Don't you think so?"

Ticos are interested and patient listeners. Asking questions about the local area and customs is a good way to get a conversation going. Be diplomatic—Costa Ricans feel insulted if foreigners criticize their culture. They are perfectly aware of the negative aspects, which they confront on a regular basis. They are interested in your country, too, so that is another safe subject. In fairly formal conversations, such as with a business associate, or with an elderly person, the polite and respectful *Usted* form of address is used instead of the more friendly *tu.*

TELEVISION

Just about every Costa Rican household, no matter how humble, has a television. During the dry season, Ticos prefer to spend their free time outside, but during the rainy season many people turn to the TV for entertainment. Day and night soap operas, or *novelas,* pervade the screen. Most of them are from South America or Mexico, and draw a large crowd of faithful fans. Imported sitcoms and other shows from the United States are dubbed in Spanish. There are also a few popular national sitcoms. The national news programs often show explicit violent incidents, as well as having good in-depth investigative reporting. Many people form their political views from what they see and hear on TV. All the TV shows are rated for violence and sex.

There are several private VHF stations, including Canal 4, 6, 11 Repretel, Canal 7 Teletica, and Channel 2 Conexion, that broadcast music videos twenty-four hours a day. Soccer games are usually televised live and take the place of scheduled programs. Channel 13 Sinart is a public station dedicated to nonviolent programming, and offers a wide variety of interesting educational and cultural programs. A few UHF channels are available, depending on location and a good antenna. They are Canal 15 UCR, Canal 31 Cristovisíon, Canal 40 Telefides, Canal 42 Extra TV, and Canal 50 FCN TV. Cable and satellite TV are widely available and offer an enormous variety of programs. Programs in English and other languages are available through these systems.

THE PRESS

Costa Rica enjoys a relatively high rating as regards freedom of the press. There are a few controversial libel laws that some claim are too restrictive, but overall the freedom of the press is untrammeled.

Daily newspapers range from those publishing quality investigative reporting to the more sensational publications. The daily *La Nación* is the nation's largest publication, and offers good national and international coverage. *La Republica* is Costa Rica's business daily. *La Prensa Libre* and *Al Día* offer national and international coverage. The daily *Diario Extra* is at the sensational end of the range. The *Tico Times*, Central America's leading English-language newspaper, is published weekly each Friday. It covers a wide variety of national and international news of interest to residents of Costa Rica, along with Central American news, local events and columns, and an impressive classified section. Many newspapers also have online versions.

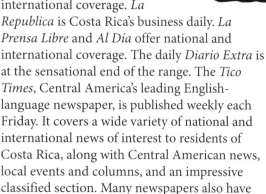

Magazines in Spanish are imported from Spain, Mexico, and South America, and English-language magazines from the USA. The Costa Rican magazine *Perfil* is popular with women of all ages for covering fashion, news of the stars, recipes, and health-related articles.

COMMUNICATIONS SERVICES
Mail

The mail service in Costa Rica was privatized several years ago, but things haven't changed much in its operation. The postal system is generally good, and relatively inexpensive. Of course there is an occasional "lost" item, or one that takes forever to arrive. The colorful stamps that decorate your postcards and letters depict a wide variety of subjects, such as flora, fauna, or the soccer team.

Post offices are generally open Monday to Friday from 7:30 a.m. to 5:00 p.m. Hours may vary somewhat from place to place. In some smaller towns the post office may close for lunch, usually from 12 noon to 1:00 p.m. On Saturdays post offices open from 7:30 a.m. to 12 noon.

There are no mailboxes on the streets; you mail your letters at the post office. Mail will be delivered to your home, though in outlying areas this may take a while. Many people take advantage of post office boxes for receiving mail. This option is quicker and more reliable, since street names and house addresses are almost nonexistent. If you receive a package that is too big for the box or to be delivered to you, you will receive a notice. Bring it to the post office desk with some identification in order to pick up your package.

Other private mail-forwarding companies are available for more security and faster delivery.

Telephone

The national telephone company, ICE, has control of all the phone lines; both landlines and the cell phone network. For international calls private carriers compete with the national company on the price.

The country code for Costa Rica from outside the country is 506, followed by a seven-digit number. Internal calls use no area code—the whole country is within the same area. Just dial the seven-digit number to make a call.

There are numerous phone booths in the city, and fewer in the outlying areas. These can be maddening to use—they are frequently out of order, and different phones use different systems. For instance, there are two kinds of prepaid phone cards with a number that you punch in, 197 and 199, and there is another type of prepaid card that you put in the phone to make a call. Phone cards are sold in stores around town. If all else fails, or you find yourself without coins or a card, call 110 to make a national collect call. This is often the easiest option.

When making a call the ringing tone is long, while the busy signal is a shorter, more rapid tone. If you want to speak, for example, to Jorge, say, "*Está Jorge?*" or "*Se encuentra Jorge?*" The standard way to answer the phone is "*Alo.*"

Cell phones operate on the same principle as anywhere else. The cell phone craze has taken Costa Rica by the reins. It is amazing how many people on the bus, on the sidewalks, or driving cars are busily talking on their cell phones. It has practically become an addiction.

Internet
Internet cafés are readily available in the cities, in tourist areas, in post offices, and in some small towns. The rates per hour are very reasonable. A growing number of Costa Ricans have the Internet available to them at their work or at home.

CONCLUSION
Costa Ricans are a cheerful, relaxed, and family-oriented people. Their generous hospitality and warmth are well-documented and enjoyed by visitors from around the world. With a strong belief in peace, they tend always to look for a diplomatic, nonviolent resolution to problems, and Costa Rica, "the Switzerland of the Americas," is respected as a democratic oasis in turbulent Central America. The Ticos are proud of their small country that has so much to offer.

It is easy to adapt to the comfortable climate and become immersed in the laid-back, outdoor lifestyle. As a business traveler you may be bothered by the casual *mañana* attitude to getting things done, but you will learn a beneficial lesson in dealing with people. Business revolves around personal relationships, so invest time and energy in this, and you will find success.

Whatever it is that brings you to Costa Rica, understanding the people and their culture will make your stay all the more worthwhile and enjoyable. Whether you are a student, on business, or on vacation, you will not fail to enjoy the "good life"—*¡pura vida!*—with the Ticos.

Further Reading

Barry, Tom. *Costa Rica: A Country Guide*. 3rd ed. Albuquerque, New Mexico: Interspheric Education Resource Center, 1991.

Barzuna, Guillermo. *Caseron de Teja*. San José, Costa Rica: Editorial Nueva Decada, 1989.

Biesanz, Mavis Hiltunen, Richard Biesanz, and Karen Zubris Biesanz. *The Ticos: Culture and Social Change in Costa Rica*. Boulder, Colorado: Lynne Rienner, 1999.

De Nuñez, Evangelina. *Costa Rica y Su Folklore*. San José, Costa Rica: Ministerio de Gobernación, 1956.

Hutchison, Peter. *Costa Rica Handbook*. Bath, England: Footprint Handbooks, 2001.

Molina, Ivan, and Steven Palmer. *The History of Costa Rica: Brief, Up-to-Date and Illustrated*. San José, Costa Rica: Editorial de la Universidad de Costa Rica, 1998.

Palmer, Paula. *"What Happen": A Folk History of Costa Rica's Talamanca Coast*. San José, Costa Rica: Editorama, 1993.

Palmer, Steve, and Ivan Molina. *The Costa Rica Reader: History, Culture and Politics*. Durham and London: Duke University Press, 2004.

Storti, Craig. *Figuring Foreigners Out: A Practical Guide*. Boston: Intercultural Press, 1999.

The Tico Times. *Exploring Costa Rica 2004*. San José, Costa Rica: The Tico Times S.A., 2003.

Spanish. A Complete Course. New York: Living Language, 2005.

In-Flight Spanish. New York: Living Language, 2001.

Fodor's Spanish for Travelers (CD Package). New York: Living Language, 2005.

Useful Web Sites

www.costarica.net
www.arweb.com/cr
www.costaricapages.com
www.centralamerica.com/cr
www.tourism-costarica.com
www.costaricanhotels.com
www.costaricaoutdoors.com
www.hotels.co.cr

www.costaricaguides.com
www.costaricaexpeditions.com
www.cinde.or.cr
www.amcham.co.cr
www.procomer.com
www.casacanada.net/arcr
www.camaracbr.or.cr

culture smart! **costa rica**

Index

culture smart! costa rica